The Psychology of Biblical Interpretation

The Psychology of Biblical Interpretation

Cedric B. Johnson

Academie Books Grand Rapids, Michigan
Zondervan Publishing House

THE PSYCHOLOGY OF BIBLICAL INTERPRETATION
Copyright © 1983 by The Zondervan Corporation
Grand Rapids, Michigan

ACADEMIE BOOKS are published by Zondervan
Publishing House, 1415 Lake Drive, S.E.,
Grand Rapids, Michigan 49506

Library of Congress Cataloging in Publication Data

Johnson, Cedric B.
    The psychology of Biblical interpretation.

    Includes bibliographical references.
    1. Bible—Hermeneutics—Psychological aspects.
I. Title.
BS476.J63   1983   220.6'01'9   83-7004
ISBN 0-310-33281-8

Edited by Ben Chapman
Designed by Louise Bauer

Printed in the United States of America

85   86   87   88   89   90 / 12   11   10   9   8   7   6   5   4   3   2

CONTENTS

Preface 7
Introduction 9

Chapter One: The Mind in Search of Meaning   17

    The Meaning of Scripture
    The Message of Scripture
    The Use of the Mind in Interpretation
    Conclusion

Chapter Two: Personality and Interpretation   41

    The Unconscious
    Cognitive Style
    Perceptual Expectations
    Creativity and Mental Sets
    The Dogmatic Person
    The Church With Half a Brain
    Conclusion

**Chapter Three: The Influence of Society
and Culture** 69

    Conflict in an Ambiguous Situation
    Public Versus Private Interpretations
    The Needs of the Group
    The Culture Gap
    Culturally Evoked Hermeneutics
    Socio-political Issues
    Culture-bound Translation
    Conclusion

**Chapter Four: A Psychological Hermeneutic
—Insight and Responsibility** 93

    The Call to Courage
    The Church—the Context for Courage
    The Call For Responsibility
    Conclusion

Conclusion 115

68651

PREFACE

Over the past few years I have had a growing suspicion that my ideas about biblical truth do not come entirely from the study of the Bible. Somehow my personal journey with the ghosts of the past, the anxieties and challenges of the present, and the alluring seductiveness of the future shapes the way I view the Scriptures. The same is true of the 'gurus' of the faith. Each one forms his or her theological system with some reference to personal psychohistory. The dispensationalists, covenant theologians, neo–orthodox people, and others cannot disguise psychohistory. *The Psychology of Biblical Interpretation* is my attempt to get behind the disguise and explain why I and other theologians, amateur and professional, come up with such divergent interpretations of the same body of truth. This is but a partial explanation. How can I as a theologian/psychologist discern the disguise of others when I do not fully know my own motivation for the writing of the present book? The discernment of the truth of the Bible is somewhat like the process of mining gold; you have to dig through tons of dirt, hard rock, and sometimes endanger your life before you discover the precious substance. I pray that the reading of the book will enable you the reader to understand and experience the great truths about yourself and the Word once again.

I am deeply grateful to my friends who have walked with me through the challenge of writing this book. Not all of them have agreed with my thesis, but all have encouraged me in the agony and ecstasy of preparing a manuscript for publication. Above all, I am grateful to Ann, my wife, and to my sons, Doran and Bevan, for giving me their love and acceptance. This environment of friends and family is truly conducive to creative endeavor. My ultimate benediction is to the God of all truth who has been revealed in our Lord Jesus Christ, the Scriptures, and the created universe.

INTRODUCTION

All is not well with the science of biblical interpretation called hermeneutics. There are many who speak with authority about the meaning and application of Scripture but the voices differ on some important issues. This book explores some of the reasons for these discrepancies in the interpretation of Scripture among Evangelicals.

The recent "battle for the Bible" has made hermeneutics a key issue in Evangelicalism today. There are different opinions about such issues as inerrancy, the role of women in the home and church, homosexuality, and social ethics.

We constantly search for objective facts that will help dispel the confusion. We look for better hermeneutical methods to help understand the truth that was delivered at Fuller, Wheaton, or Princeton, but no one seems to have the corner on the market in regards to the message of the Bible. Does such uncertainty leave us without a biblical foundation for our lives? Are we left with a skepticism that says, "Your interpretation is as good as mine even if we differ"? The answer to both questions will be a categorical no.

Although I want to affirm the authority of Scripture and state that its message is clear in matters essential to faith and practice, I also want to explore some psychological reasons for the fact that divergent interpretations exist. The impact of the subjective world of the interpreter on the reading of the Bible has been observed by many: there would be many different and contradictory interpretations. One such person, G. C. Berkouwer, writes:

> Such a variety of differing and mutually exclusive 'interpretations' arose—all appealing to the same Scripture—that serious people began to wonder whether an all-pervasive and seemingly indestructible influence of subjectivism in the understanding of Scripture is not the cause of the plurality of confessions in the Church. Do not all people read Scripture from their own current perspectives and presuppositions? Do they not cast it in the form of their own organizing systems, with all kinds of conscious or subconscious preferences, ways of selection which force the understanding of Scripture into one particular direction?[1]

The subjective world of the interpreter expressed through the mind is either the bane or blessing of hermeneutics. It constructs and tests theories; it may, however, also distort the truth.

The theme of the book is that there are no uninterpreted facts in the study of the Bible. "The Bible says" has been claimed as support for slavery, apartheid, nuclear arms proliferation, sexism, and a host of other unjust systems. To use facts, theories, and observations to prove a biased perspective is intellectual dishonesty. Differences due to bias among biblical interpreters are not often the result of a conscious twisting of the facts; nor are they due to a lack of scholarship on the part of the interpreter. However, there are some general principles about bias in human perception that apply. The intent of this book is to explore and define the way interpreters view the Scriptures from unique and more or less biased perspectives. Suggestions are also offered as to what we can do about it.

J. Robertson McQuilkin paints a negative picture of the role of the behavioral scientists as those who have moved in and soon may take over the task of biblical interpretation. He feels that we are in a precarious position and asks, "Is the drift in the way evangelicals understand Scripture merely part of the larger popular shift of authority to the new high-priestly cult of the psychologist and his bloodbrothers, the sociologist and the anthropologist?"[2]

I am not writing this book to state that a psychologist is a high priest with an inside track on the meaning of Scripture. However, God has given order within His creation and we do use our minds to formulate theories about all the things we observe. Although the Bible is the final authority on faith and practice, it needs to be interpreted, and there are psychological factors involved in that process of interpretation. This book is offered as an analysis of the function of the mind in the process of interpretation.

In chapter 1, "The Mind in Search of Meaning," the psychological processes *within* the mind of the interpreter are examined. An important distinction is made between meaning and application of Scripture, and the way the mind functions in respect to each of these. The human mind is more than a lens that must be focused on the truth. It has the ability to construct models, test theories, see parts in relation to the whole, and exercise disciplined creativity. A theory of the mind is important for hermeneutics. Behavioral scientists have given us an extensive data base for theories about how people interpret the world around them. The formation of models, or theory building, can be a helpful part of the discernment of truth in Scripture. Hermeneutics *is* a science. The quest for meaning in the biblical text is a quest for validity. How do I know that my interpretation is the correct one? It must be explored by means of dynamic theoretical blueprints, creativity, theory testing, and theory change. We need to interact with God's Word. This chapter intends to develop an awareness of how our theoretical frameworks are affected by preunderstanding. However, realizing the potential for bias in interpretation should not and must not cause us to jettison our models.

The influence of personality factors in the possible distortion of the intended meaning of the Scripture is discussed in chapter 2, "Personality and Interpretation." I believe that hermeneutics can learn from the behavioral sciences. The psychology of the individual is explored with reference to studies of the unconscious motivational processes, cognitive styles, perceptual distortions, creativity, and dogmatism. Such theoretical information can be helpful in the explanation of apparently contradictory interpretations of Scripture that exist within Evangelicalism.

In chapter 3 "The Influence of Society and Culture on Interpretation," the interaction between the person and society is discussed with reference to bias in interpretation. Cultural conditioning can create a gap between the interpreter and the text, especially in ambiguous or difficult passages. In most instances, however, the best hermeneutical tools enable scholars to discover the meaning of the text. Group influences on the interpreter are discussed—the needs of the group, public and private interpretations, and conflict in an ambiguous text. Culturally evoked interpretations and culture-bound translations are examined as causes of interpretative bias.

Chapter 4 presents the concept of "A Psychological Hermeneutic—Insight and Responsibility" Various illustrations of distorted or conflicting interpretations are given with the message, "If the shoe fits, put it on!" The fear that inhibits creative but orthodox interpretation is discussed together with options for responsible action.

The sooner we recognize both the assets and the problems of human involvement in biblical interpretation, the better. In expounding the problem of interpretative bias Thiselton says, "No one expounds the Bible to himself or to anyone else without bringing to the task his own prior frame of reference, his own pattern of assumptions which derive from sources outside the Bible."[3] This is a challenge to interpreters to seek greater personal understanding of their own biases. Unless such psychological awareness is sought as a necessary prelude to hermeneutics, there will be no real progress toward the unity of the faith.

> Peary relates that on his polar trip he traveled one whole day toward the north, making his sleigh dogs run bruskly. At night he checked his bearings to determine his latitude and noticed with great surprise that he was much further south than in the morning. He had been toiling all day toward the north on an immense iceberg drawn southwards by an ocean current.[4]

The iceberg of unconscious motivation and other psychological factors needs to be heeded, surveyed, and mastered in the hermeneutical task. Northward movement with respect to the objective constants needs to be seen in the light of personal and cultural factors. But we do not walk alone. We have the Spirit of truth within our lives. Our fellowship is with Him and together we can move beyond subjective distortions in the interpretive process and experience the joy of being set free by His truth.

NOTES

[1]G. C. Berkouwer, *Studies in Dogmatics: Holy Scripture* (Grand Rapids: Eerdmans, 1979), p. 106.

[2]J. Robertson McQuilkin, *Problems of Normativeness in Scripture: Cultural versus Permanent.* Paper presented to the International Council on Biblical Interpretation, 1981, p. 2.

[3]A. T. Thiselton, *The Two Horizons: New Testament Hermeneutics and Philosophical Description* (Grand Rapids: Eerdmans, 1980), p. 114.

[4]J. O. Gasset, *Meditations on Quixote* (New York: Norton, 1961), p. 104.

ONE

The Mind in Search
of Meaning

1

This chapter proposes a description of the mind from the perspective of the behavioral sciences. It is important to understand the processes of the mind in the interpretation of the Bible. This will help us to formulate, develop, and modify theories of biblical interpretation. We will discuss how the mind participates in the quest for meaning and application. It tests hypotheses, builds theories, and acts as an executive that creatively adds to and sometimes changes existing theories of interpretation.

Let us begin with the Scripture. We must distinguish between meaning and application, describe the relationship of the parts of Scripture to the whole, and deal with personality involvement and the Word of God.

THE MEANING OF SCRIPTURE

The meaning of Scripture represents the truth-intentions of the divine author. It is grounded in the fact that Scripture is "God-breathed" (2 Tim. 3:16). God intends to communicate His mind and will in a rational, verbal message. Walter C. Kaiser, Jr., describes that meaning as "that which was to be found in a text as indicated by its grammar, the author's use of his words, and his truth-intentions."[1] The meaning of the message has not changed since "men spoke from God as they were carried along by the Holy Spirit" (2 Peter 1:21). Why then all the confusion over meaning? Why are there so many different and conflicting interpretations of Scripture in Christendom? Does the meaning of the Bible exist only in an ideal but unreachable sense? Hermeneutics wrestles with these and other questions. A clear distinction must be made between meaning and application.

As we seek a biblical perspective on nuclear war, genetic engineering, divorce, homosexuality, and the ordination of women, the significance of Scripture emerges through application. The God-breathed Word *is* profitable for faith and life but personality and culturally conditioned biases impact the interpretative task. Sometimes the meaning does not get through to us, or if it does, it is garbled.

I want to state at this point that I am not assuming widespread confusion in the discovery of the meaning and application of Scripture in regard to the central doctrines necessary for faith and practice. I work on the assumption that we can have an adequate (although not complete) knowledge of the meaning of the central issues in Scripture. There are different human interpretative responses to that final and authoritative meaning, but the meaning preceded our involvement with the Bible. "God is love" has a meaning accessible to both author and interpreter. We can't make words mean anything we want them to mean. The discovery of meaning in the Bible should not be like the use of a projective personality test like the Rorschach, in which various inkblots stimulate the unique psychological world of each person. The same inkblot may stimulate one person to see a prehistoric monster, while another may see the aftermath of an explosion in a paint factory. Yet, there is a sense in which the subjective and private world of the person defines the interpretation so that the meaning of the text varies from person to person. Such subjective interpretation is a distorting factor that deserves consideration in biblical hermeneutics.

THE MESSAGE OF SCRIPTURE

The idea that the Bible has a clear meaning was enunciated by the Reformers, who spoke of the *perspicuity,* or clarity, of Scripture. What they meant was that the Bible is sufficiently clear in its basic message of salvation by grace through faith and in setting forth the basic guidelines for living the Christian life. An example of the early church's attempt to set forth the perspicuity of Scripture is seen in the Apostle's Creed. Such theological statements cover central issues like the Virgin Birth of Christ and his bodily Resurrection. According to Alan Johnson, "No ancient or modern cultural information can contravene these basic affirmations."[2]

Not only did the Reformers write about the clear message of Scripture but they also spoke of the type of person that could hear and understand the message. To them the "meaning" of the Bible was not just available to professionally-trained theologians adept in the original biblical languages; the clear meaning was available to all Christians. The Reformers saw that there are large sections of the biblical message relating to faith and practice that are sufficiently clear to all Christians. We need not regress to a point in history where the Bible was chained to the pulpit and written in a foreign language that only priests could understand. John Wycliffe and other Bible translators have given the common people access to the message of Scripture. I do not intend to demean the scholarly work of biblical interpreters who study the original biblical languages, wrestle with theological issues, scrutinize linguistic and archaeological evidence, and with each succeeding year lead us to a better understanding of the Bible. I am simply making a case for the ability of the common person to understand the meaning and application of central salvation and practical issues.

Although the basic message of Scripture is abundantly clear, not all of Scripture is easily understood by every casual reader. There are many difficult and disputed passages. It is here that the perspicuity of Scripture is clouded and thus open to greater differences in interpretation. This then presents the task for hermeneutics: to expound on the meaning of Scripture by means of exegesis, synthesis, and application.

The flow from meaning to application is similar to the flow of a river. The task of hermeneutics is to map the river. The meaning has a divine source expressed by human instruments through language, personality, and culture. At the source, the meaning is single and unchanging. It is discoverable through *exegesis* and *synthesis*. It then flows along a changing riverbed (different applications to different cultures), and produces life in its recipients.

Exegesis analyzes the words (in their context) of the human authors. The grammatical-historical method of interpretation examines, among other things, the linguistic, cultural, and historical background to the inspired writings. At the point of exegesis comparatively few differences arise over meaning—a verb is either active or passive and the syntax follows standard rules of grammar. Even though there are a host of unfinished tasks in biblical exegesis, such as in linguistics and archaeology, most of the distortions of meaning occur in the two final stages of interpretation, synthesis and application.

Synthesis, the task of theologians, is the process of "gathering up, and surveying in historically integrated form, the fruits of exegesis."[3] At the point of the theological analysis, hermeneutical models are built and tested. The structure for each model arises from the essential unity, or organic character of the data base, the Scriptures. As with any science, we don't have perfect models but only close approximations to the ultimate model inherent to the Scripture. The examination of the theory-building capacities of the human mind is the subject of chapter 2.

For the time being I will view the meaning of the Scripture as that which emerges in the process of exegesis and synthesis. It is possible for an interpreter to miss the meaning because of an incomplete use of the grammatical-historical method, invalid synthesis and theory building, and unwitting theological myopia. However, most distortion comes in the application of meaning.

This, then, is the third stage of hermeneutics, *application*. At this point we seek to address the age-old questions of humankind from a biblical perspective. This is the most complex and troublesome part of developing a sound hermeneutic. It is mostly in the area of synthesis and application, especially in relationship to peripheral issues, that our inadequate interpretations emerge. The hermeneutical process involves: exegesis, synthesis, and application.

Interpretation, as an endeavor of the human mind, presents the opportunity for the mind to shape, influence, color, or even distort the true meaning of Scripture. Although no one would subscribe to a "mindless" biblical interpretation, few biblical interpreters seem to incorporate a description of the functioning of the human mind in their system of hermeneutics.

THE USE OF THE MIND
IN INTERPRETATION

When I view my television set, I accept the product, the program, with little technical understanding of what goes on inside the 'box.' But when the sound or picture vanishes, my "black-box" approach does not help me solve the problem. Problem solving requires a knowledge of the inner workings of the electronic device.

The discovery of meaning and significance in Scripture is a process that has some similarities to the discovery of the inner workings of a television set. Exegesis, synthesis, and application cannot be treated in a "black-box" manner. The operations and inner workings of the human mind need to be understood if we are to have an accurate hermeneutic. The exact nature of the human mind has been debated by philosophers, theologians, and scientists for centuries. I will not revisit that debate except to say that I am attempting to view the mind from a biblical perspective. The Bible does not view the person as someone who *has* a body and a mind but rather as someone who *is* mind and body. Frederick Buechner reflects a biblical view of persons when he writes, "the body and soul which make up a man are as inextricably part and parcel of each other as the leaves and flames that make up the bonfire."[4]

The "immortal soul" concept is Greek. In contrast, the Bible reflects the unity of the person, and presents the doctrine of the resurrection of the body. God prizes our bodies so much that Jesus became flesh and dwelt among us. He will bring us back to live not as some disembodied echo of a human being but as a complete person. The body and soul will be united in resurrection splendor. In the biblical view then we don't *have* minds, we *are* minds. Medical science, both ancient and modern, with its emphasis on psychosomatic medicine recognizes the essential unity of the person. A sick mind makes for a sick body. A lengthy illness can cause depression.

To say that the mind is involved in the interpretation of the Bible is to place emphasis on a particular expression of our person through our mental faculties. How then do we know that a person is expressing personhood through mental abilities? Understanding the functions of the mind is vital to an understanding of biblical hermeneutics.

God communicates His Word and works, which are interpreted by thinking beings. In interpretation the mind does not act like a camera that merely records details. The mind acts as an *executive process* that orders its perceptions. We show selectivity and favoritism toward the biblical data. Such an executive process develops in early childhood and, according to Mussen, Conger, and Kagen,

> is firmly in control of cognitive functioning by the time the child is 10 or 11 years old. The functions of this executive process are to monitor and coordinate his perceptions, memory, and reasoning processes, to relate past experiences and future possibilities to the present, to select the best strategies to solve a problem, and to permit the child to be self-consciously aware of his own thinking.[5]

The mind is, of course, actively involved as the person seeks to make sense of the data. This process allows us to formulate hypotheses. The end result of hypothesis testing is an integrated intellectual framework which provides a general explanation of phenomena. Such a general framework has been variously termed a theory, schema, or paradigm.

Hypothesis Testing

Hypothesis testing occurs in biblical interpretation as well as in "pure" science. The process begins with the intellectualizing of the problem. The data base that is observed is the biblical text, extrabiblical evidence from history, linguistics, cultural norms, and a wide variety of other sources. The accumulated observations are related to each other in a logical manner. A hypothesis is then formulated. F. N. Kerlinger describes this hypothesis as "a conjectural statement, a tentative proposition, about the relationship between two or more phenomena or variables. Our scientist will say, if such-and-such occurs, then so-and-so results."[6]

The testing of hypotheses is a process we engage in every day. Some of our efforts are scientific; some are informal. I might reflect that *if* I continue to lounge in front of the T.V., *then* I will waste my mental powers, not write this book, compromise my moral standards, and suffer all the other evils that are supposed to come with chronic T.V. viewing. This reflection represents a tentative attempt at hypothesis testing. Sometimes the conclusions we posit in our hypothesis testing have far-reaching consequences. For example:

> *If* the mustard seed is not the smallest of all seeds as Jesus said it was, *then* the Bible is not accurate in details of science.

How we make our mental movement from the *if* to the *then* determines the validity of our answer, shapes our theology, and in the end, directs our lives. Let us examine the "if-then" sequence in hypothesis testing by considering the assumptions behind the premise of the argument. The best logic is useless if our assumptions about the premise are wrong. In the example of the mustard seed, who says that the mustard seed is not the smallest of all seeds? Jesus may have been speaking of the smallest seed in Israel, the smallest in the whole world, or simply the smallest seed in common knowledge. The Bible is not reflecting an error; the error is in our faulty assumption. Hypothesis testing, therefore, involves tentative but testable statements about facts and the relationship between them.

We all develop theories of why things are the way they are. These theories range from speculative guesses (there is human-like life on other planets), to systematic, controlled, critical, replicable studies of how people behave in stressful situations. The best science (including hermeneutics) seeks to avoid guesses and give the best possible explanations for a particular phenomenon. These attempted explanations are theories. A theory has been defined by Kerlinger as "a set of interrelated constructs (concepts), definitions, and propositions that present a systematic view of phenomena by specifying relations among variables, with the purpose of explaining and predicting the phenomena."[7]

The executive process organizes the data from hypothesis testing into what Piaget calls *schemata*. The cognitive unit of the schema has been defined by Mussen, Conger, and Kagen as:

> The mind's way of representing the most important aspects, or critical features, of an event. The schema is neither an image nor a photographic copy, but rather like a blueprint. Like all blueprints, it preserves the arrangement of and relations among a set of significant elements.[8]

Here is a dramatic illustration of the innate ability of persons to form schema. Isolated Indian children in the mountains of Guatemala who had never seen paper, line drawings, or photographs before were shown line drawings that merely suggested a familiar object like a fish. Each child had to guess the object that was being suggested. On the whole, the Guatemalan children did no worse than American children. All guessed correctly 80 percent of the time that the figure represented a fish. These schemata are a description of data organized and tested in the human mind. They are the smaller building blocks of human knowledge. We may even call them *microtheories.*

The human mind can only hold a few items of data in relationship to others at one time. Think for instance of how much you as the reader remember of this chapter at this moment. With what other data are you associating these thoughts? Your schemata are small bits of knowledge. Computers can instantly recall a wider range of associated data.

If a schema is to be of value to science it must be stated in the form of a hypothesis. From early childhood on, we state, test, modify, or change our schemata continually. We share our findings with each other; we "show and tell" in the first grade and later write erudite scientific journals. Soon the microtheories become global descriptions (*Macro*-theories). Others have called such pervasive categories of thought *paradigms.* Richard Gelwick, for example, describes them as,

> the configuration of beliefs, values, and techniques by which normal science is pursued. It represents the outlook and methods by which a discipline of study conducts its routine life, interprets data, and does research. A paradigm provides metaphors, analogies, explanations, and standards for solutions to puzzles.[9]

Schemata and paradigms function as interpretative

frameworks that are testable. They are the essence of our presuppositions in biblical interpretation.

An example of a schema would be the ideas associated with the "good shepherd' image in the Gospel of Luke. The schema of the care of the shepherd for the sheep becomes the structural framework the mind uses to organize related ideas like God's love for His people. A paradigm, on the other hand, is a more comprehensive model of truth. Other paradigms used by the church are: the fundamentals of the faith, the inerrancy of Scripture, and systems of interpretation such as dispensationalism or covenant theology.

The process of formulating an intellectual construct such as a theory, schema, or paradigm involves other aspects of mental functioning. These include seeing the part and its relationship to the whole, and being aware of personal involvement with the subject.

The Parts and the Whole

There is a danger in viewing the Bible as an encyclopedia. An encyclopedia has many facts but most of them are unrelated. Some people seem to view the Bible as a series of unrelated verses. Such a totally atomistic approach to biblical interpretation would be rare, but a faulty or incomplete understanding of context is a common problem of interpreters.

The view of some Christians that spanking is the main form of discipline for children mandated by the Bible is based on a single verse without proper consideration of the view of discipline and relationship to children as treated in the Bible. A study of the term *rod* shows that it represents more than an instrument of punishment. A "proof-texting" approach is a poor way to discover the meaning of Scripture. A Christian theory of child rearing should be based on systematic and complete studies of the meanings of individual words, the climate of parent/child relationships, the nature of the children and the function of rewards. The unity of the Bible, therefore, forces us to recognize the interrelatedness of its parts.

The roots of such a faulty hermeneutic are to be found in the misapplication of the methods of hypothesis testing set forth by Francis Bacon (d. 1626) and the scientific work of Isaac Newton (d. 1727). The movement in their logic was from the particular to the general. Mark Noll demonstrates how the Newtonian method has been misapplied in interpretation. He writes:

> Why do evangelicals read the Bible as we do? Is it not at least possible that it is Baconianism— rather than a principle of Scripture itself, that has encouraged some evangelicals to regard the Bible as a compendium of separate facts and commands rather than as a unified revelation of the character and acts of God? Discussions over the ordination of women sometimes illustrate this tendency. In addressing this issue, are we not prone to hurling individual texts at one another (Gal. 3:28; I Tim. 2:12), instead of examining the general character of God's dealing with his people from Genesis through Revelation?[10]

Some Evangelicals cling tenaciously to the methods of Bacon and Newton. They continue to be convinced, in words of Noll, that "reliable knowledge arises from the accumulation of renewed facts apprehended directly by objective observers."[11] There are other methods in science whereby truth is discovered, and Bacon and Newton are not the last word. Theological systems cannot be constructed merely by piling one fact on another without reference to the unified message in the Bible. A mere list of Bible references at the end of an argument or theological statement does not necessarily reflect accurate exegesis or synthesis. We should not believe that the validity of a position depends on the number of verses cited.

The position that a good scientist does not just pile one fact on another to prove his/her position or move only from the particular to the general was established by the Gestalt[12] school of psychology in Germany in the 1920s. Max Wertheimer (1880–1843) presented an alternative view of reality that the whole is different from the sum of its parts. To Gestaltists, perception is always in the context of what is presented. The whole, the configuration, and field of organization are important to the perception of reality.

One underlying assumption of Gestalt psychology is that there is not a one-to-one correspondence between the data we pick up with our senses and what we actually perceive. They believed that we interpret the world around us only in the way our minds are capable of perceiving it. There is a difference between the perception of an object and the object itself. The mental connections, the associations, the insights we have, explain our interactions with and formulations of reality. A pure Gestalt approach to biblical interpretation could lead to a circular argument since the particular can't be understood without the whole and the whole is in the mind of the interpreter who makes various cognitive associations. Meaning is only realized, then, in the mind of the interpreter.

The biblical message, however, has a unity of its own, and the Gestalt position alerts us to this fact that a particular text has meaning not only in its own right but also in relationship to the whole of Scripture. Our minds relate to the whole because God has given us the ability to make such associations and integrate the particular with the general. Creativity in biblical interpretation will be discussed later, but theology as a human science expounds how the parts of the Bible relate to the whole. No one part of the Bible speaks of God existing as Trinity. However, the whole picture presented in Scripture is of a Triune God: Father, Son, and Holy Spirit. Such a statement comes through the integration of the independent verses about God's existence, self statements, incarnation, and indwelling. We first experience God, and then "tell the world" with our personal theological statement.

The formulation of a doctrine of the Trinity utilizes our ability to associate one idea with another. Not many orthodox theologians would disagree with such an argument. There are some issues, however, where there would be disagreement among interpreters. How do those who adopt a "no remarriage" position for Christian divorcees, relate their interpretation of Matthew 19:9 to the more general idea that it is not 'good for man to be alone' (Gen. 2:18)? To what state should we banish the divorcee: adultery (in remarriage) or loneliness (in remaining single)? Tough questions like these can't be answered with reference to a verse like Matthew 19:9, which has a variety of interpretations. The answers we derive from our logical arguments (hopefully with the correct premise) have far-reaching personal implications. We must not merely hear the Word—we must also obey it. Obedience involves a high level of personal commitment.

Personal Involvement in the Truth

Newton encouraged movement from the particular to the general in science. He also presented the position that the scientist could not have a personal involvement in the subject. His emphasis was on observable facts whose characteristics are entirely independent of our opinions about them. All personal considerations have to be eliminated from the investigation. And so the true scientist weighs, measures, and puts things into test tubes and does not get personally involved in the experiment. Theology from a purely Newtonian perspective is done in a detached, "objective" manner. Such a process, however, leads to sterility of thought, dry orthodoxy, and a false dichotomy between subject and object.

The *Institutes* of John Calvin, the *Dogmatics* of Karl Barth, and most of the classics in the history of theology were written by people who were deeply involved with their subject (God and His Word). Their minds were fired with the truth that was already there. The Bible has an existence of its own and we cannot have a detached objectivity in our understanding of its message. It comes alive in us as we hear its message and obey its precepts and principles. My personal experience of truth is vital to discovery. I am not subscribing to a position that the Divine Word *becomes* truth as I experience it. It was always His Word. However, my subjective involvement with the message makes it real to me.

Part of an interpreter's involvement with the Word relates to the Holy Spirit's application of its precepts and principles to life. He is the one who convicts of sin, leads into all truth, and points to Christ. Without the inner activity of the Spirit a person could not even begin to understand the Scripture.

Sterile objectivity (lack of personal involvement with the study) has been sharply criticized by Michael Polyani. He ridicules the whole idea of scientific detachment and points out that we cannot disregard the active involvement of the knower with the known. Such a way of gaining meaning is a radical departure from Newton but is vital today. This involvement of the interpreter will lead in one of two directions:

1. The data can be distorted in terms of the personality and sociological conditions of the interpreter. This issue will be explored in chapter 2 and 3.
2. The data can be integrated, organized, and systematized by means of the creative involvement of the interpreter with the text. The whole process of interpretation, from the consideration of single words to the creative involvement of the interpreter in the whole picture, ends in the construction of theories. This process is examined in the remainder of this chapter. Once a theory, schema, or paradigm has been formulated and accepted by the individual and/or by a more general audience, it can still undergo change. Two distinct processes that allow a theory, schema, or paradigm to develop and change have been called by Piaget *assimilation* and *accommodation*.

Assimilation occurs when information from the environment is received and changed by certain "sets of rules" for thinking. As Mussen puts it, "In simple language, assimilation is applying old ideas and old habits to new objects and viewing new events as part of existing schemata."[13] The new data that presents itself to the person in assimilation does not change existing schemata, but merely adds details. The meaning of a verse, for example, can remain the same with the assimilation of new data.

Accommodation, however, is a radically different process. In response to additional data, the schema or theoretical framework in the mind of the interpreter changes.

Assimilation can be likened to the process of food ingestion. Accommodation, however, is like digestion and the resultant physical change.

Theories develop and change at both the individual as well as the societal level. Piaget talked about changes of schemata in individuals. Popper talks about changing "procedures." Thomas Kuhn points to a theory of change in the history of science in *The Structure of a Scientific Revolution*. Both Kuhn and Popper are speaking of more global changes at the societal level. Polanyi also pointed to more global changes and called them paradigm shifts.

At both the individual (Piagetian) and societal (Kuhnian) levels, new theories are developed when the old ideas (schemata, paradigms) no longer meet the demands of a new situation (new discrepant data). The person or system is placed in a dilemma. A choice can be made to change the old theory (interpretive structure) or maintain the status quo. Scientific revolutions occur when old paradigms break down and new ones are developed to take their places. The change in the science of astronomy from a geocentric to a heliocentric view of planetary motion is an example of a paradigm shift.

How is it that in one instance a shift will occur and in another it will be inhibited? I will attempt to answer the questions with reference to the science of hermeneutics with creativity highlighted as one of the cognitive processes.

Creativity and Change in Theory

Creativity produces changes in paradigms and schemata. But is this creativity? For some an image of a Bohemian artist in Paris flinging blotches of paint randomly on a canvas is conjured up. Not so for investigators of the structure of the human intellect and theories of cognitive functioning. One of the major contributors to research on creativity has been J. P. Guilford. He presented the concept of divergent thinking that included specific subprocesses like word, ideational,

33

associational, expressional fluency, and originality. E. P. Torrance defines creative thinking as, "a process of becoming sensitive to problems, deficiencies, gaps in knowledge, missing elements, disharmonies, and so on: Identifying the difficulty; searching for solutions, making guesses or formulating hypotheses about the deficiencies, testing and retesting these hypotheses, and finally communicating the results."[14]

Tacitly held theories, assumptions, and opinions in hermeneutics and other sciences often contain seeds of error or discrepancy. The creativity of the interpreter may contribute to the solution or to the dilemma. The cumulative effect of a series of contradictions in the text may lead the investigator to "imagine why there are differences." The divergent thought processes evident in such a dilemma can be a form of creativity. The fluency of ideas and frequency of alternative solutions will soon impact the interpretation process.

In general, then, a creative person is willing to take a chance in problem solving. He or she is not afraid of new ways of looking at the data. Creative insights help an interpreter break out of a box and ask questions, see relationships, and build models that can later be scrutinized and tested by others.

What then is an example of a truly creative idea in biblical interpretation? Geoffrey Bromiley points out that, "Original thoughts both orthodox and heterodox have an uncanny knack of being 'original' many times in many different generations.[15] There is "nothing new under the sun." The Martin Buber distinction between God and "it" and God as "he" in the I-Thou-It relationships had its antecedents in the thought of Friedrich Schlegel nearly one hundred years before. Bromiley concludes, "Creativity is in any case harder to achieve or to find than is often imagined."[16]

A truly creative thought is certainly not a "form of subjective impressionism in relation to its object."[17] God's self-revelation is the object of study for the biblical interpreter. We cannot interpret the Scripture as our fancy pleases; God defines Himself and His work. The Bible will set limits on our creativity and so will the stage in the process of interpretation at which we choose to be creative.

Earlier biblical interpretation was defined as a threefold process: exegesis, synthesis, and application. Each stage of interpretation is open to different degrees of creativity. The task of each stage is on a continuum of convergent and divergent thought. Convergent thought relates to a way of thinking that is in concert with the data base itself. Divergent thought relates to creativity.

Exegesis demands less creativity and more convergent thought. The tense of a verb, the syntax of a sentence, the genre of a piece of literature, and the cultural setting of a letter all have an established data base. Granted, the work of linguistics and archaeology is incomplete and there are texts that provoke endless discussion, but by and large exegesis requires little divergent thought.

In the interpretative states of synthesis and application creative thought is most evident and most required. This does not mean, however, that there are no rules or procedures for these processes. They are defined by Scripture itself. All Scripture is God-breathed; there is organic unity. There is a connectedness with the historical development of theology. Packer describes the process as "the exegetical circle."[18] He writes: "If his exegetical procedure is challenged, he defends it from his hermeneutic; if his hermeneutic is challenged, he defends it from his doctrine of biblical authority; and if his doctrine of biblical authority is challenged, he defends it from the texts."[19]

At all times God's self-revelation provides a test of the validity and internal consistency of any dogmatic system or hermeneutical theory. Creative interpretations are always under the authority of the Word. However, there is still room for original thought. For instance, the distinction between specific (local) and universal applications of Scripture requires much creative insight.

In chapter 3 an examination will be made as to why such creative processes are inhibited in any science. Suffice it to say at this stage that creative insight is an integral part of both schematic changes and paradigm shifts. We need creative prophets and innovators who will address themselves to discrepancies within some orthodox positions. We need persons who will go beyond the Baconian scientific work that is filled with replicative work that only supports the status quo.

CONCLUSION

The active involvement of the person of the interpreter was seen to be essential to the discernment of the message of Scripture. The meaning and application of the message is discovered in the process of exegesis and synthesis of the text. Despite interpretive difficulties, the clear message of the Bible is available for the life and walk of faith.

The science of hermeneutics needs to note the operations of the human mind. The mind works as an executive process formulating and testing hypotheses and theories. Microtheories are viewed as schemata and macrotheories as paradigms. The essential parts of theory formulation are:

1. The person's ability to relate parts to the whole
2. The personal involvement of the interpreter with the text.

Theories are changed through the processes of assimilation, accommodation, paradigmatic shifts, and the creative involvement of the interpreter with the theory. Our minds certainly do not respond to biblical interpretation like sponges to liquid. We do not just soak in the truth; we actively process it.

NOTES

[1]Walter J. Kaiser, "Meanings From God's Message: Matters for Interpretation." *Christianity Today,* October 5, 1979, p. 30.

[2]Alan Johnson, *A Response to: Problems of Normativeness in Scripture: Cultural Versus Permanent,* (Paper presented to the International Council on Biblical Interpretation, 1981), p. 11.

[3]James Packer, "Hermeneutics and Biblical Authority," *Themelios,* Autumn, 1975, *1:1,* p. 6.

[4]Frederick Buechner, Wishful Thinking; A Theological ABC [1st ed.] (New York: Harper & Row, 1973), p. 41.

[5]P. W. Mussen, J. J. Conger, and J. Kagan, *Child Development and Personality* (New York: Harper and Row, 1974), p. 277.

[6]F. N. Kerlinger, *Foundations of Behavioral Research* (Chicago: University of Chicago Press, 1970), p. 12.

[7]Ibid., p. 9.

[8]Mussen, *Child Development,* p. 271.

[9]Richard Gelwick, *The Way of Discovery: An Introduction to the Thought of Michael Polanyi* (New York: Oxford University Press, 1977), p. 55.

[10]Mark Noll, "Who Sets the Stage for Understanding Scripture?" *Christianity Today,* May 23, 1980, p. 17.

[11]Ibid., p. 17.

[12]The foundational thought behind the Gestalt School of Psychology was that in our perception of the world the whole is more than the sum of its parts.

[13]Mussen, *Child Development,* p. 40.

[14]E. P. Torrance, "Education and Creativity," in C. W. Taylor (Ed.), *Creativity, Progress, and Potential* (New York: McGraw-Hill, 1964), p. 6.

[15]Geoffrey Bromily, "Evangelicals and Theological Creativity," *Themelios,* September 1979, p. 5.

[16]Ibid., p. 5.

[17]Ibid., p. 5.

[18]Packer, "Hermeneutics," p. 6.

[19]Ibid., p. 6.

TWO

Personality
and Interpretation

2

In chapter 1 we explored the nature of the task of biblical interpretation and how the functioning of the mind allows us to successfully and often creatively address this task. The mind is obviously a great gift enabling us to explore the Word and know our God.

But it is not all that neat and simple. The voices of biblical interpreters do not well up together in a single united chorus of agreement. There are many different and conflicting interpretations of Scripture.

The Bible is not an ambiguous stimulus. We are not thrown back on our subjective impressions. The Bible is able to make us wise unto salvation through faith in Christ Jesus and teach, rebuke, correct, and train us in righteousness (2 Tim. 3:15−16). There is a clear message for all who would hear and obey. Why then is there a fog of confusion amongst some interpreters regarding certain key issues in the application of that meaning?

For the last decade I have watched and wondered why there are so many contradictory theological positions in Evangelicalism. One biblical commentary will persuade me to accept covenant theology with its practice of infant baptism. Another erudite scholar seeks to persuade me that baptism is for believers only. Historically, churches split over the day of worship, the ordination of women, integration, and the use of musical instruments in worship. Today we seek biblically informed answers to equally difficult questions, such as, nuclear war, homosexuality, genetic engineering, and divorce.

My contention is that conflicting theological positions are in part due to the fact that we all approach a text, sacred or secular, with our strong subjective biases. Even though we have a commitment to read the Bible on its own terms; and even though we want the Divine and human authors to speak for themselves, somehow we still come up with contradictory views on some issues. Why? In this chapter and the next, we will take the role of the behavioral scientist and explore some of the personal and cultural factors that influence the interpreter in his or her application of the meaning of the text.

Most people are familiar with the idea of "seeing" what you want to see or viewing a situation through "colored glasses." The assumption is that our perceptions of the real world can be distorted at times. Another way of viewing biased interpretation is as a process where truth is "filtered" through the person's unique qualities.

Personal uniqueness, bias, and the process of how we perceive the world around us can fall under the general title of Personality. There is both semantic and theoretical confusion about the definition of *personality*. I will use the term in a very general sense to indicate the relatively enduring and important characteristics, both conscious and unconscious, observable and unobservable, that exert a strong influence on an individual's behavior.

The behavior I seek to explore is that of biblical interpreters as they engage in the exploration of the meaning and application of Scripture. The biblical data are sometimes distorted through the "spectacles" of our personality.

What causes bias in the way people interpret the data of the world around them? Is it a matter of different perspectives as in the reports of persons who view an accident? Do people have unconscious biases in their perspective? Are there such factors as different cognitive styles where *different* is not necessarily wrong?

THE UNCONSCIOUS

Part of this bias may stem from what has been termed "the unconscious." Among psychologists, there is no agreement about the role and influence of the unconscious or unobservable emotional states on conscious behavior. At one end of the continuum, B. F. Skinner, a strict behaviorist, feels that it is unnecessary and misleading to account for mental illness or pathological behavior by positing the existence of unobservable emotional states.

Cognitive behavior therapists and researchers continue to demonstrate the place of mediating cognitions in human behavior.[1] They demonstrate that our thoughts affect our behavior. However, their emphasis is on conscious thought that exists in our immediate awareness. Psychodynamic theorists like Freud go a step further to say that there is a "beyond the awareness" dimension of cognition.

Sigmund Freud (1856–1939) compared the mind to an iceberg with conscious processes represented by the tip. Most levels of awareness operate unconsciously; they are like the rest of the iceberg below the surface. He developed his theory of the psychological unconscious on a two-fold basis:

1. His clinical observations of patients who reported bothersome conditions for which there was no plausible explanation or control.
2. His theoretical presuppositions about the nature of persons derived from Darwin's evolutionary theory with its emphasis on instinctual biological drives. The biological drives form an infrastructure of human thought, and according to Robinson, these drives "have been raised to the level of a medical or neurological reality. The engine of psychological growth is energy, which behaves according to the same sorts of laws prevailing in the physical world."[2]

Freud may have erred in his fretful attempt to fit his observations of neurotic patients into his theories. His ratio of facts to assumptions may not have been balanced. However, we cannot rob his observations of all their validity, especially when other theorists have emerged with evidence that unconscious forces play a significant part in human behavior.[3] Furthermore, we don't have to accept his presupposition relating to evolutionary and instinctual biological drives in order to posit the existence of unconscious forces. Freud was observing real people with problems that had an unconscious etiology. Something *was* happening to his patients in terms of thought processes beyond their awareness or control.

The recent review of Howard Shevarin and Scott Dickman supports Freud's position. Shevarin and Dickman define the unconscious as "that class of psychological events that are at the time unknown to the patient but that actively affect the patient's behavior."[4] The authors cite three sources of evidence in support of the psychological unconscious: namely selective attention, subliminal perception, and certain visual phenomena involving perceptual processing.

In considering biblical interpretation from a psychological perspective then, which position shall we choose? Generations of scholars in the field of hermeneutics have recognized the influence of preunderstanding on interpretation. C. S. Lewis observed that "what we learn from experience depends on the kind of philosophy we bring to experience."[5] This traditional pattern of integrating hermeneutics with psychology, which places a strong emphasis on the psychodynamic theories of Freud and others, has been rejected by some (notably Hirsh).[6] Let us use this pattern and examine the potential impact of unconscious processes on biblical interpretation.

What can Freud say to biblical interpreters? The answer could well be: "Be cautious about the impact of your unconscious processes on the application of meaning." Unconscious processes are manifested in reaction formation, selective attention, and a transference relationship with the text. We will consider each of these in turn.

Reaction Formation

One of the functions of the unconscious mind is the management of certain anxious thoughts. The mind uses various devices to deal with anxiety; these are described by psychodynamic theorists as unconscious defense mechanisms. A person may distort reality in attempting to reduce anxiety. One such defense is *reaction formation,* which may take two forms: 1) the person may fight actively against the thing that provokes anxiety; 2) the reaction of the person is just the opposite of what he/she is really feeling. A homophobic person who actively crusades against homosexuals may be defending against his or her own homosexual impulses. The crusader for prohibition could be defending his or her unconscious fear of substance abuse, or impulse control.

To suggest that every time a person had a strong feeling or behaved aggressively in a certain direction, he or she was attempting to reduce anxiety with a reaction formation would be reductionistic. However, one wonders about the motivation of persons who overreact. Believing that an attitude of overreaction to homosexuality, for example, would not affect one's interpretation of Scriptures that deal with homosexuality would be naïve, and to say that the person is manifesting a reaction formation defense against the fear of homosexuality is unwarranted. We may suspect a reaction formation in the person who says, "God could not be opposed to anything so fulfilling as homosexual love," or who proceeds to explain away all comments in the Bible against it. Such a person could be defending against the anxiety-provoking thought that homosexual behavior is in fact a dysfunctional expression of one's sexuality.

Selective Attention

Selective attention is another aspect of the psychological unconscious. Shevarin and Dickman point out that, "Inherent in all the major models of attention is the assumption that at least part of the cognition related to attention takes place outside of awareness."[7] Ongoing psychological processes are affected by these beyond-the-awareness cognitions. Evidence for the latter comes from experimental studies rather than clinical observations. The fact that a person attends to one issue and neglects another has wide support. The issue under discussion at this point relates to unconscious influences on selective attention. We need to be aware of ex post facto decisions that rule absolutely *why* a person has interpreted a passage of Scripture in one way and not another. After-the-fact psychological explanations can be notoriously inaccurate and open to hindsight biases. David Myers writes:

> In our psychological society a speculative
> psychology-of-the-gaps pops up everywhere to
> explain human behaviors not yet explainable
> scientifically. Oedipal interpretations of
> homosexuality, existential theories of the
> popularity of Star Wars, and psychodynamic
> explanations of Richard Nixon's enigmatic be-
> havior are offered to a public that can hardly be
> expected to discriminate psychology's hunches
> from its established facts.[8]

The problem with psychodynamic concepts such as
selective attention, the unconscious, and reaction formation is that they are not subject to many types of scientific
investigation.

Note that, at this stage in modern American culture, to say that a phenomenon is unscientific is tan-
tamount to saying that it is absolutely wrong. The word
science exercises the kind of authoritative sway that the
Christian religion did during the Puritan era of American history. Richard Gelwick writes: "Events and ideas
have combined to convince the modern world that the
objective ideal of knowledge is the method of science
and hallmark of truth, even though it is not practiced in
science nor capable of establishing truth."[9]

Even behaviorists cannot maintain a scientific position that includes total objectivity. They have chosen a
methodology that responds only to observable behavior
and refuses to make inferences about unconscious motivation. There are environments other than the
laboratory where unconscious processes can be observed. The relationship between the patient and his or
her psychotherapist is one such context.

The Text and Transference

Psychotherapists describe the unconscious and

stereotyped ways by which a person relates to the authority symbol or person as transference.[10] Such an interpersonal perceptive distortion causes a person to relate to an authority "as if" the relationship were part of an early childhood conflict. Some therapists recognize and utilize the "as if" quality of the relationship between them and their patients as a part of the psychotherapeutic process. Often the patient transfers to the therapist feelings that the patient experienced towards a significant authority figure in childhood. Just how certain therapists utilize the transference phenomenon is not my immediate concern, but the results of tranference must be noted. A developmental perspective helps us understand transference. A child learns the experience of trust in the first six months of life. If, for some reason, the child was deprived of a nurturing relationship with the primary care giver during that period, the experience of trust in later life becomes severely disturbed. As an adult, such a person may be inhibited in intimacy, doubt the best intentions of others, distrust authorities (including the Bible) and generally feel insecure. They relate to the authority "as if" it were the care giver from the past. Such a patient, deprived of childhood experiences of trust, may distrust his or her therapist.

Different childhood experiences of authority produce different adult conflicts. Some adults manifest a passive surrender to superior power. They have a series of unquestioning responses to authority symbols and persons. A classic Candid Camera television show illustrated such compliance to authority symbols. A traffic signal was placed in the middle of a sidewalk near a busy shopping center. A number of parcel-laden persons would stop on the sidewalk when the signal was red. There was no logical reason for their behavior except for their unquestioning compliance with a symbol of authority—the traffic signal.

The fact that the Scriptures are authoritative in their meaning and in our lives needs to become a part of the mind set of all believers. However, the term *authority* provokes different images and responses in different people. Psychotherapists recognize that some people have problems with authority. Of these, some become very compliant in the presence of an authority, others rebel against symbols and people of authority. The Bible is authoritative, but for some people it evokes the wrong image of authority. They have an unconscious response to the Scriptures as if they are being taught by authority figures from their past. They are not relating to the Bible like the Bereans in Paul's day, who "examined the Scriptures every day to see if what Paul said was true" (Acts 17:11). Their reflexive response sometimes distorts the true meaning of Scripture.

Consider the effect of transference on biblical interpretation. One person may respond to the Scripture rebelliously because it tells him or her to behave in a certain manner. Another person may respond with unquestioning compliance to the scriptural applications of an authority figure (e.g., the preacher). In both instances, compliance and rebellion, the real meaning of the Scripture could be distorted by an unconscious transference relationship.

No matter, then, how a person chooses to approach the phenomenon of unconscious motivation, we all approach our world with a unique legacy of learned responses. Whether we call these "unconscious responses," or see them as aspects of our person that we choose to ignore, they can impact the process of biblical interpretation.

Transference is not the only manifestation of reflexive responses to past events. We all have painful events in our past that impinge on the present. Take for instance the development of our feelings toward the

49

term "father." For some the term evokes feelings of warmth, affection, and acceptance. When they come to the Scriptures and read that God is their father, they have a positive response. However, for others the term evokes a negative response. J. B. Phillips recognized such interpretative distortions in his excellent book, *Your God is too Small.* [11] God may be viewed as a policeman who is out to get us. The genesis of such distortions is often to be found in a person's developmental history. Take the case of the Christian woman who views God as a distant and judgmental parent. Her developmental history reveals such a relationship with her father. During her teenage years her father became afraid of the incestuous thoughts he was having. Instead of dealing with his thoughts he defended himself against them by distancing himself emotionally from his daughter. The child experienced this defensive act as personal rejection. When she became a Christian she transferred this fear to her heavenly father. Her interpretation of Scripture was therefore distorted through such an unconscious response. One can only wonder about the events in a person's past that lead to an overemphasis on such things as the holiness or the love of God. Could not whole systems of theology have been impacted by such unconscious transference?

In a similar fashion, each of our cognitions is unique—a derivative of our learning and our biological makeup. Let us go on to examine how different cognitive styles can affect biblical interpretation.

COGNITIVE STYLE

The statement, "It's all a matter of how you look at things" may be highly relevant to how people interpret Scripture. Is it a matter of pure chance that some people approach the Word in a highly analytic and logical manner and others are more adept at global analyses? Why are some interpreters creative, while others follow conventional patterns only? How do we account for different learning styles among interpreters? The behavioral sciences provide a data base on different cognitive styles that provide some answers to these important questions.

In studies of different cognitive styles in approaching and transposing information, H. A. Witkin and others have demonstrated two approaches, *field independent* (analytic) and *field dependent* (global). Leonard Berkowitz describes the experiment as follows:

> The apparatus for a rod and frame test includes a luminous square frame that may be tilted either left or right and a luminous rod that is in the center of the frame but independent of it. In a darkened room, the subject is required to adjust the rod to an upright position with the frame remaining tilted. To be successful, the subject must be able to ignore the frame and refer to his own body position. If the tilt of the rod is large, the subject is said to be dependent on the visual field; if small or 'upright,' the subject is independent of the field.[12]

The persons with an analytic cognitive style have no trouble "disembedding" a rod from its context (the frame) perceptually. Persons with a more global cognive style manifest difficulty in isolating detail from context. V. Mary Stewart commenting on such studies writes: "All of these systems share in common the notion that there is some kind of tension, or polarity, between the objective, the analytic, the rational . . . and the subjective, the synthesizing, the intuitive."[13]

Note that *pure* "global" or "analytic" types are few and far between. However, a person or group may be predominantly one or the other. Stewart[14] and Theodore T. Y. Hsieh[15] have applied Witkin's findings to different cognitive styles within the church community. Both of the writers built their case on the basis of Bernard Ramm's[16] distinction between Spirit- and Word-oriented Christians.

*Word-*oriented persons are more analytic. They emphasize the meaning of scriptural texts, formulate systems of theology, and in Christian living are rational, articulated, and objective. Stewart writes: "The 'Word' concept encapsulates the rational, articulated, objective aspect of the redeemed Christian life, whose lynch-pin is the unchanging standard of Scripture and its rationally evolved theologies."[17]

*Spirit-*oriented persons are more global and intuitive in their cognitive processes. The emphasis is on personal experience in the Christian life. Interpersonal issues are more important to the Spirit-oriented person. God and His Word are to be experienced rather than rationally analyzed.

The ideal for the Christian life, according to Ramm, is a balance in the relationship between the Word and Spirit. The history of the Church reveals periods when the balance was lost. Sometimes reactions to one extreme produce another extreme. For instance, Søren Kierkegaard, in reaction to the dry orthodoxy of his day, propounded a religion that is to be experienced (Spirit). He overreacted to the "letter" that killed in presenting an alternative where the "Spirit" gave life. Stewart[18] points to trends within modern Evangelicalism where exponents of the letter (Word specialists) are persons like Francis Schaeffer and John Montgomery. Spirit-oriented persons are represented by writers such as Oswald Chambers. Schaeffer, Montgomery, and Chambers are not extreme examples like Kierkegaard where there is a major loss of balance between Word and Spirit. However, they are representatives of different cognitive styles. *Different* does not mean "bad" or "heretical" provided that there is a recognition that a balance between the two must be manifested.

Evidence that the two types of cognitive styles are to be found within Evangelicalism today was demonstrated experimentally by Theodore Hsieh.[19] He tested the Witkin experimental procedure on eighty-two undergraduates at a theologically-conservative Christian college. He utilized a sixteen-item, forced-choice questionnaire with polar questions such as:

a. In my own personal Bible study times, I spend more of my time concentrating on finding the correct interpretation of Bible passages, even going to commentaries once in awhile for further insight (word-oriented statement).

b. In my own personal Bible study times, I spend more of my time reading for inspiration and strength to meet present problems.[20]

He found that there was a statistically significant relationship between Word-oriented Christians and field independence over and above Spirit-oriented Christians and the same factor.

What then do the theoretical reflections of Ramm and Stewart and experimental findings of Hsieh indicate to the process of biblical interpretation? It may well be that the intuitive interpreters are field dependent and the positivists are field independent. Not that we would discover persons at the extremes of the spectrum. In most cases those would only represent "straw" people set up for contentious debators and writers. However, hermeneutical systems like dispensational theology may appeal to persons that have field independent cognitive styles. By the same token a system of interpretation like relational theology may appeal to field dependent persons. Is this then a case of "East is East, and West is West, and never the twain shall meet"? No. We need both perspectives as we interpret the Scriptures and we need to make them relevant to life. We need the corrective of other cognitive styles to keep us from the extremes of positivism and intuitionism.

PERCEPTUAL EXPECTATIONS

The way a person interprets a situation is in many ways shaped by the memory of similar events. I may, for example, hear a truck outside my suburban home early some Monday morning and assume that it is the regular Monday garbage collection when it is not. We call on past experience to interpret present events. Psychologists who study the phenomenon of memory present the theory that we store general and typical ideas of frequently encountered stimuli. Such storage leads to the development of a prototype or model. Kagan and Havemann write of such a process that:

> When we encounter a new stimulus we can identify it immediately because it resembles the prototype. Then we note the special features that distinguish this particular new event, making it similar to but different from all other events that also fit the prototype.[21]

The development of cognitive models lends itself towards persons having a "mental set" towards an environment. Laboratory experiments have demonstrated the effect of such mental sets on subsequent perceptual interpretations. Figure 1 illustrates such an experiment. Do you see a person or a rat in the final drawing of each set?

Figure 1

A Little perceptual magic: now it's a man, now it's a rat

For a startling demonstration of how perception is affected by expectations, cover both rows of drawings, then ask a friend to watch while you uncover the faces in the top row one at a time, beginning at the left. The friend will almost surely perceive the final drawing as the face of a man. Then try the bottom row in similar fashion on another friend. This friend will almost surely perceive the final drawing as a rat. The psychologists who devised this experiment found that 85 to 95 percent of their subjects perceived the final drawing as a man if they saw the other human heads first, as a rat if they saw the animals first—though of course the final drawings are exactly alike.

The application of such research on perceptual distortion to the process of biblical interpretation can be illustrated in a number of ways. A person may be influenced over a period of years to interpret a verse in a particular manner. For instance, many interpret the passages in Ezekiel 28:12–19 and Isaiah 14:12–14 to be a reference to the fall of Satan. But was the "morning star" (Isa. 14:12) really Satan? Why is it that some read "Satan" instead of Lucifer (Isa. 14:12, KJV)? Could it be a mental set that each one brings to the passage that informs the interpretation? Some would look to the archaeological evidence of near Eastern mythology and see that the Lucifer concept refers to a scoundrel who happened to be the king of Tyre. Others working from the mental set that Satan fell interpret Lucifer as Satan. In both cases "Lucifer" is an ambiguous stimulus because of the interpretive difficulty. We go to our prototypes to explain new and ambiguous situations. The realization that our perceptions can be shaped by mind sets should help interpreters to be less dogmatic in their conclusions about passages of Scripture that present interpretive difficulties. How then do we break up these interpretive log jams? The next section will explore the issue of creative problem solving.

CREATIVITY AND MENTAL SETS

In chapter 1, the creative processes whereby old paradigms are changed was explored as well as the cognitive processes of assimilation and accommodation. What causes such change to be inhibited at the societal and individual levels? What has happened to creativity in biblical interpretation? Mental sets have certain advantages in helping us with everyday problems. We can drive to work or fix breakfast without thinking about what we are doing. However, such sets partially account for the fact that creative thinking is so rare. Some psychologists point out that even among really intelligent people as few as one percent are really creative. Why is this the case? E. P. Torrance[22] has exposed certain factors in American society that tend to inhibit creativity in children. Success orientation makes children prefer to stay within the given structures of society in order to succeed. They fear failure if they try something new or unknown. The conformity to the peer group and social pressure, which begins when the child is in about the fourth grade, shows itself in a demonstrable drop in most children's creativity. There is a reluctance to explore, ask questions, and use their imagination because teachers often discourage such behavior.

Home life can also enhance or inhibit creative thought in children. Dreyer and Wells[23] found that parents of creative children allowed decision making and freedom of social exploration at an earlier age. On the other hand, other researchers like Sheldon[24] found that restrictiveness and hostility on the part of parents tended to inhibit creativity in children. The profile of the creative person (one with a breakaway mind that influences generations of scholars) has been well described by Howard Gruber. He studied the lives of creative people like Darwin, Einstein, and Newton and sketched out the nature of their creativity.[25] He went beyond the traditional view that creativity is either a personality characteristic or a mental ability. This view emphasizes either nonconformity or divergent thinking. Gruber described the creative person as one who (1) pursued his/her work with a passion and persistence; (2) grows in his/her ideas over the years; (3) uses nonverbal phenomena such as imagery to develop a conceptual framework (Albert Einstein, for example, at the age of 16, imagined himself as riding a beam of white light, which became the basis of later theoretical formulations that led to the theory of relativity); and (4) deals with anomalies and problems in his/her system in a unique fashion. The problematic issue is put aside, bracketed, and the person goes on to work in areas where the problem is solvable. Take the example of Newton. He postulated the existence of the force of gravity. The anomaly in his system was that such a force required the influence of one body over another sometimes at a great distance. Gruber writes that this was

> a strange idea that he didn't like more than anyone else did. He suspected the cause would have

something to do with the inner structure of matter, but it was too early to find out—not enough was known at the time about the structure of matter. So, in effect, he bracketed the problem.[26]

The creative person is often a lonely prophet who operates at the margins of his/her discipline or culture. The standard problems of peers are bracketed as he/she juggles seemingly unrelated ideas with joy, persistence, and ease. Social pressures call for the person to conform to orthodox ways of problem solving. The social rewards for the creative process are small.

Social pressures, combined with a need to conform, stifle creative biblical interpretation in many institutions of learning, from elementary schools to seminaries and universities. The fear of censure by a person's peers often inhibits creative problem solving. We tend to see things the way others do because we want their approval. We are also sometimes afraid to make mistakes. Such issues will be explored in some depth in chapter 3, which suggests solutions to the enhancement of creativity and the modification of bias in interpretation.

THE DOGMATIC PERSON

An individual personality characteristic that may militate against an accurate interpretation of Scripture is dogmatism. Note that dogmatism is not to be equated with a firm conviction regarding one's faith. Dogmatism is not the "Here I stand" of Martin Luther, but is a personality characteristic that manifests a lack of balance between conviction about one's principles and openness to new insight.

A situation that might elicit a dogmatic response in hermeneutics would be, for example, an interpretative ambiguity. If the facts of the passage are not clear and do not seem to fit an interpretative framework, a person may feel threatened by the ambiguity. Things must be clearly defined—certainly true or certainly false. In this situation, a dogmatic person becomes very anxious. How can he or she solve the dilemma of the ambiguous interpretation? Behavioral scientists Milton Rokeach and T. W. Adorno have established a similar profile of the behavior of dogmatic or closed-minded persons.[27] Leigh Shaffer elaborates how we can discern whether a person is behaving dogmatically.[28]

1. He or she chooses to refer to the opinion of some chosen authority to solve the interpretative dilemma. The "authoritative" statement may come from a former mentor, seminary professor, or significant church leader. The "commentaries say" is usually a reference to the views of esteemed leaders on one side of the theological spectrum. The dogmatic person refuses to read Karl Barth's position when Cornelius Van Til is the chosen authority on a given problem.

   These people are, according to Shaffer, "Threatened people who manufacture personal security by abducting their freedom of thought and action to a few trusted authorities whom they follow loyally."[29]

2. Oppositive views to those of the *authority* are viewed as dangerous, heretical, or unorthodox. There is an overly simplistic polarization of the "good guys" and the "bad guys".

3. Such people live in a constant dilemma of wanting to have a balanced cognitive framework. Conflicting and threatening aspects of reality are desired for the sake of the need to know and understand most certainly.

The above presentation of the dogmatic person represents an extreme position. The community of biblical interpreters rarely has an extreme dogmatic "straw person" available for our scrutiny.

Shaffer attempts to demonstrate that Harold Lindsell's *Battle for the Bible* is an example of dogmatism. Evangelicalism is replete with ex post facto explanations of Lindsell's controversial book. W. S. La Sor feels that Lindsell was angry with Fuller Theological Seminary because he was not given the presidency of that institution. The speculation is interesting but inconclusive, since Lindsell does not meet all the major criteria of the dogmatic person.

Divergent opinions on numerous issues are evident in Evangelicalism today. *Mild* forms of dogmatism do exist. If one of the characteristics of dogmatism is the view that "I am most certainly right and you are most certainly wrong" then dogmatism is being manifest when, according to Carl Henry:

> *Christianity Today* under Harold Lindsell polarized the inerrancy camp and Fuller Seminary polarized the errancy camp into mutually exclusive rivalries that admit little conversation.[30]

A close scrutiny of evangelical commentaries in ambiguous passages will soon reveal whether the writers are manifesting a degree of closed mindedness.

Do such persons take into serious account the views of people from other theological camps or do they listen selectively only to chosen authorities? Such is the case, when, according to Shaffer, they "Confuse their estimate of authorities with their grounds for belief in the authority's statements."[31] In biblical interpretation the ultimate authority is the Word of God and no one person has the final word on any theological issue. Our theological "heroes" and "villains" pale in the light of the authority of Scripture.

I have discussed individual personality character-istics that may contribute towards preunderstanding in hermeneutics. The *cause* of such bias is not really known. We may argue whether nature or nurture has contributed towards the particular characteristic. In the end the answer may be found in a dynamic interaction between the person's inherent and acquired character-istics. However, one side of the issue that is both cul-tural and physiological relates to the use of the two sides of the human brain.

THE CHURCH WITH HALF A BRAIN

The old saying that "the left hand does not know what the right hand is doing" may be applied to cogni-tive processes in hermeneutics, with reference to the two cerebral hemispheres. It could be said that, in a sense, the church in the Western world uses only half its brain—a position that will be supported by the evidence to follow.

Brain research points to differences in cognitive functioning. The left hemisphere of the brain has cus-tomarily been seen as better suited for analytic ap-proaches to problem solving. The right hemisphere operates more holistically and globally in conceptual or-ganization. We thus have two functionally differentiated information-processing subsystems. Don Tucker mus-ing on the implication of such differences writes: "It is difficult to contemplate this view of the brain without wondering what the implications are for such tradition-ally enigmatic features of human nature as creativity and psychopathology."[32]

The concern of the present work is more that of laterality and creativity in hermeneutics.

The famous studies by Nobel Prize winner Roger

W. Sperry on the cognitive function of "split-brain" patients in California helped demonstrate the subtle psychological differences between the two cerebral hemispheres. Each patient had the corpus callosum severed as a treatment of choice for intractable epilepsy. Joseph E. Boger, one of the surgeons involved in the operation, found that the left hemisphere was predominantly propositional and the right hemisphere appositional. The one was logical, convergent, and analytical; the other was intuitive, divergent, and helped the person experience his or her world in terms of a gestalt, or whole.

However, a review of the research data indicates conflicting findings for the notion of hemisphericity. Both sides of the brain *are* involved in the various human functions including thought. However, persons may differ according to a predominant style of processing information.[33]

Even the whole notion of creativity, once thought to be a uniquely right brain function, involves both hemispheres. There are both verbal and nonverbal components of the creative enterprise. For instance, artists with right brain lesions were able to create and paint without major impediment to their task.[34]

A strong case for cultural differences in a hemisphere dominance is made by Robert E. Ornstein in his book *The Psychology of Consciousness*.[35] He presents the thesis that the "left-hemisphere" modes of Western society have suppressed the development of right hemispheric functions. Whatever the source of cognitive styles we still cannot deny their existence and differences.

We also note the significant difference between theologizing in the West and East. Much of Western systematic theology has arisen in a philosophical context where precision of expression and sharp cognitive focus were the guiding principles. Charles Taber contrasts that the Eastern churches "opted for the most part to give expression to their faith via other types of symbols: liturgical language and ritual, iconic objects, and the like."[36] The differences between the theology of the West and East has been described by Wallace Chafe and Charles Taber as the difference between concepts and mental images.[37]

Concept	Mental Image
Abstract	Concrete
General/universal	Specific/particular
Analytical	Holistic/Gestalt
Linear	Multi-dimensional
Rational	Affective
Evokes cognitive knowledge	Evokes intuitive knowledge
Sharply narrowing focus	Broadly evocative focus
Univocal	Multiple layers of meaning

In biblical interpretation, therefore, the East is better suited, by virtue of their cultural conditioning and cognitive style to interpret passages that deal with images, metaphors, anthropomorphisms, parables, and texts that demand an affective response. Taber writes:

> There is no reason to assume that, if Christianity had arisen and first become dominant in an Asian or an African setting, Christian theology would have taken the philosophical road at all. Certainly, a theology developed in the non-western world would not have been so nakedly intellectual, so deficient in affective impact, as ours commonly is.[38]

In biblical application, the difference between the East and West can be highlighted in a similar manner. A colleague of mine who taught for a year at a seminary in the Philippines points to the preference of the Asian students for Old Testament passages. The students related better to the story of Abraham than the logical, linear, and analytical argumentation of St. Paul to the Romans. I realize at this point that the boundary between individual (hemisphere dominance) and cultural differences is somewhat blurred.

CONCLUSION

The process of biblical interpretation requires the use of the whole person. In some phases of the interpretative process the "left brain" functions (logical thought) are prominent—for example, in the exegesis of the text. The rules of grammar are logical and there is not much room for divergent thought. The later stages of interpretation, namely, synthesis and application, are certainly not beyond logic but require more of the functioning of the right brain. The ability to grasp the whole picture in relationship to a particular doctrine or issue in Scripture requires creative thought. Theory building in systematic theology is an example of such divergent abilities to see the whole as well as the part. The essential unity and authority of Scripture insures that the part (e.g., exegesis of a particular verse) is not divorced from the whole. Hermeneutics that is true to its source, the Scripture, is not a "split-brain" procedure. We are to pursue the hermeneutical task with both sides of the brain in both historic branches of the church.

NOTES

[1]The proponents of such an approach as that of Albert Ellis, Aaron Beck and Donald Meichenbaum seek to determine what thought processes may be self-defeating to a person, and get the person to stop thinking such thoughts and start thinking more constructive thoughts.

[2]D. N. Robinson, *An Intellectual History of Psychology* (New York: Macmillan Publishing Co., 1981), p. 382.

[3]Freud is an illustration in the realm of scientific endeavor where presuppositions controlled the interpretation of data. An excellent analysis of his

philosophical antecedents and biases is found in Daniel N. Robinson pp. 376—91.

[4]Howard Shevarin and Scott Dickman, "The Psychological Unconscious: A Necessary Assumption for all Psychological Theory," *American Psychologist,* May 1980, p. 422.

[5]C. S. Lewis, *Miracles* (New York: Macmillan, 1947), p. 11.

[6]E. D. Hirsch, *Validity in Interpretation* (New Haven and London: Yale University Press, 1967).

[7]Shevarin and Dickman, "The Psychological Unconscious," p. 423.

[8]David G. Myers, *The Inflated Self* (New York: Seabury, 1980), p. 105.

[9]Richard Gelwick, *The Way of Discovery: An Introduction to the Thought of Michael Polanyi* (New York: Oxford, 1977), p. 15.

[10]The idea that a person can experience a transference relationship with the text of Scripture was first presented to me by a student, Lee Erickson, in 1980.

[11]J. B. Phillips, *Your God is too Small* (New York: Macmillan, 1953).

[12]Leonard Berkowitz, *A Survey of Social Psychology* (Hinsdale, Illinois: Dryden Press, 1975), p. 552.

[13]V. Mary Stewart "Cognitive Style: North American Values and the Body of Christ." Proceedings of the 21st Annual Convention, Christian Association of Psychological Studies, 1974, p. 263.

[14]Stewart, Cognitive Style, p. 260

[15]Theodore T. Y. Hsieh, "Cognitive Styles and Word versus Spirit Orientations among Christians" *Journal of Psychology & Theology,* Summer 1981, p. 175.

[16]Bernard Ramm, "The Way of the Spirit," *HIS,* 1974, *34* (6), pp. 16—18.

[17]Stewart, "Cognitive Style," p. 260.

[18]Stewart, "Cognitive Style," pp. 259—69.

[19]Hsieh, "Cognitive Styles," pp. 175—82.

[20]Hsieh, "Cognitive Styles," p. 178.

[21]J. Kagan and E. Havermann, *Psychology: An Introduction* (New York: Harcourt, Brace, Jovanovich, 1980), p. 302.

[22]E. P. Torrance, "Torrance Tests of Creativity Thinking: *Norms,*" Technical Manual (Princeton, New Jersey: Personell Press, 1966).

[23]A. S. Dreyer and M. S. Wells "Parental Values, Parental Control, and Creativity in Young Children," *Journal of Marriage & Family,* 1969, *28,* pp. 319—37.

[24]E. Sheldon, "Parental Child Rearing Attitudes and their relationship to cognitive functioning of their pre-adolescent sons," Unpublished Doctoral Dissertation, Syracuse University, 1968.

[25]Howard Gruber in "Breakaway Minds, Howard Gruber Interviewed by Howard Gardner," *Psychology Today,* July 1981, pp. 64—73.

[26]Gruber, "Breakaway Minds," p. 69.

[27]Dogmatism is not just due to dispositional characteristics in people. Situational variables are involved in dogmatic behavior. The experiments of Stanley Milgram sought to determine how people respond to authority (a situation variable). He found that less dogmatic (authoritarian) people refused to obey the experimenter (the authority) when he or she gave the command to give another person in the experiment an electrical shock.

[28]L. S. Shaffer, "Dogmatism, Openness and Faithfulness in Theological

Debate," *The Bulletin,* 1981, vol. 7, No. 2, pp. 5—9.

[29]Ibid., p. 6.

[30]Carl Henry, "The Cultural Relativizing of Revelation," *Trinity Journal,* Fall 1980, p. 142.

[31]Shaffer, Dogmatism, p. 6.

[32]Don Tucker, "Lateral Brain Function, Emotion, and Conceptualization," *Psychological Bulletin,* January 1981, p. 19.

[33]M. C. Corballis, "Laterality & Myth," *American Psychologist,* March 1980, pp. 284—95.

[34]O. L. Zargwill, "Thought and the Brain," *British Journal of Psychology,* 1976, *67,* pp. 301—14.

[35]R. E. Ornstein, *The Psychology of Consciousness* (San Francisco: W. H. Freeman & Co., 1972.)

[36]Charles Taber, "Is There More than One Way to do Theology?" *Gospel in Context,* January 1978, p. 7.

[37]Wallace Chafe, *Meaning and the Structure of Language* (Chicago: University of Chicago Press, 1970).

[38]Taber, "Is There More than One Way to do Theology?" p. 7.

THREE

The Influence of Society and Culture on Interpretation

3

In our better moments we are aware of the fact that no person is an island. We cannot isolate ourselves from the influence of our environment. Social psychology is the study of our interaction with people and the world about us and is defined as "an attempt to understand . . . how the thought, feeling, and behavior of the individuals are influenced by the actual, imagined, or implied presence of others."[1]

Social influences on the way we view reality, especially in relationship to biblical interpretation, are developed in the present chapter. Undoubtedly the areas in the behavioral sciences that contribute most to the understanding of the distortion of information are social-psychology and anthropology. David Myers points to studies that demonstrate how our beliefs control our memories and interpretations. He writes, "evidence for this truth is standard fare for introductory courses in psychology. Numerous demonstrations illustrate that what students will see in a picture can be influenced by what they are led to expect."[2] How people handle ambiguity, discrepant beliefs, the needs of the group, and general cultural influence are examined with reference to actual distortions of biblical meaning.

The understanding of social influence on hermeneutics is a truly interdisciplinary venture. Anthropologists like Charles R. Tabor and Charles Kraft will help broaden our understanding with their writing on cultural influences on biblical interpretation. In all we will be pressed into the examination of the validity of our own hermeneutics. At times the 'clear' picture will not be available and we will encounter internal conflict. Such conflict may indicate personal bias in interpretation.

CONFLICT IN
AN AMBIGUOUS SITUATION

Each person can tolerate a certain degree of ambiguity. The level of toleration can reflect the person's maturity as well as the degree to which she or he values the opinions of the group. A person with a low self-image and a high need to please others conforms easily to group pressures. Studies on social conformity by psychologists M. Sherif and Solomon Asch demonstrated experimentally that an ambiguous situation produced various responses in people.

The classic experiments were with the so-called auto-kinetic effect. Each subject was taken into a dark room and made to observe a stationary dot of light on the wall. In such an ambiguous situation the person was asked by Sherif to estimate how far the light moved. When the subject made a decision in a group of people, which sometimes included confederates who exaggerated the extent of the movement, he or she showed a high degree of conformity to the group opinion. There have been numerous variants on the 1937 Sherif study, e.g.,

Solomon Asch, but all of them contribute to our understanding of social conformity. The experimenters concluded that:

1. If the person values the opinion of the group and he or she is made to feel like a deviant, the rate of conformity with group opinion will be high.

2. Cohesive groups have a greater chance of getting people to conform to their opinion on judgment.

3. The person's conformity increases with an increase in the degree of ambiguity of the situation.

4. Persons with low self-esteem are more likely to conform to the group decision.

5. Sometimes there is a marked difference between the person's private opinion about the ambiguous situation and his or her publicly-stated opinion.

To point to a one-to-one relationship between the social conformity studies and the process of biblical interpretation would be impossible, however. For instance, the issue of whether light moved or did not move was not personally important to each subject. However, it *is* important to biblical interpreters whether their stimulus (the biblical text) means one thing rather than another. But, even in a matter as important as interpretation, some degree of social conformity may occur.

The application of the science of hermeneutics in the formulation of theologies gives evidence from time to time of ambiguous situations and social demands that tempt the interpreter toward conformity. For example, an interpreter may come to the conclusion that equalitarian relationships in the home or church are true to the biblical data. He or she may then encounter an ambiguous interpretative issue like whether the word *head* means "source" or "authority." Assume that there is no other data to inform the interpreter and that on the weight of the evidence she or he leans toward an equalitarian philosophy. This finding is contrary to the traditional view of his or her church, which believes in "hierarchy" and the "chain of command." The person with a low self-esteem who greatly values the opinion of the group will change his or her conclusion and bring it into line with the teaching of the church. "Head" is therefore consistently interpreted as "authority." The fault for such an inadequate solution lies in the group's rigid opinion and the person's lack of courage to stand for her or his conviction.

We like to experience consistency in our thinking. Holding conflicting ideas and theories in our mind at the same time on *important* issues is difficult. For example, an individual's theological position may sanction the remarriage of a divorcee, but the individual's church may adopt a hardline "no remarriage" position. Such dissonance calls for scientific investigation.

The studies of Leon Festinger and others indicate that people prefer to be in a state of cognitive consistency especially when on important issues. Also, the more we suffer for a particular position the more likely we are to hold to it despite dissonant cognitions. Sometimes the intensity of the pain (criticism, church splits, etc.) serves to petrify a particular belief. The tenaciousness of certain persons toward their theological position in the face of contradictory evidence may well reflect the blood, sweat, and tears of old battles. The difficulty the person had in joining the group may also be reflected. For instance a particular church group makes it difficult for people to join because of stringent doctrinal requirements. The group may have rigid, legalistic requirements for Christian living. In order for the person to join the church, he or she must give up several worldly practices. Each requirement would be justified scripturally by the group. After a person had joined such a church, he or she would have difficulty interpreting the Scriptures differently from that of the group. In the case of an ambiguous situation or dissonant cognitions, that person must choose between membership in the group or the assertion of a divergent opinion.

Some groups allow for a degree of theological diversity in their midst but usually only with persons who have won their trust, or with persons who have already gained prestige (e.g., a popular author) and who function well within the bounds of the group norms. Such individuals accumulate idiosyncracy credits. We give our theological heroes some rope. With the same rope we hang our theological serfs.

There is much pressure toward intellectual and behavioral conformity in certain groups. Many times one group will break away from its parent body on the premise of a defense of orthodoxy. Many years later the splinter group will be defending the old position despite new theological insights and different world issues that require new applications of Scripture. The breakaway group expends a great deal of energy defending old positions, castigating those who emerge with new issues, and always demanding of its followers that they be theologically correct. In such a context, church members listen to sermons and constantly ask the question, "Is it right?" rather than "What does the Word of God say to me?"

What then happens to dissenters within orthodoxy? Do they keep their dissenting opinions to themselves and conform to the orthodoxy of their group? Or do they speak out prophetically?

PUBLIC VERSUS PRIVATE INTERPRETATIONS

When the dissenter begins to doubt his or her orthodox, theological convictions, what are the options? There are at least four: 1. He or she can sell out to the group for fear of rejection. 2. He or she can allow the group to persuade him or her to change a belief despite a personal view to the contrary. 3. He or she can maintain a private conviction while publicly espousing the orthodox belief. 4. He or she can publicly affirm his or her "unorthodox" conviction and sever the relationship with the group.

Let us begin a consideration of public versus private interpretations by asking how authority (the church) can affect the interpretation of the Scripture?

Roman Catholics and Protestants debate the meaning of 2 Peter 1:20, "No prophecy of Scripture came about by the prophet's own interpretation." G. C. Berkouwer writes of this verse:

> To the present day there has been much difference of opinion regarding this inclusive claim. Roman Catholic exegesis sees it as containing a contrast between independent and ecclesiastical exegesis. It is taken to be a prime source of justification for the decree of Trent that it is the church's right "to judge regarding the true sense and interpretation of holy Scriptures."[3]

Even though most Protestants believe the verse is a warning against arbitrary exegesis and in no way excludes individual interpretations, the pressure to conform with denominational interpreters is great. Many times a denomination does not have a creed or official exegesis of a topic or verse, but the person is pressured to conform to a certain interpretation. The latter is true whether there is an official (e.g., Episcopal) or unofficial (e.g., Baptist, Church of Christ) hierarchy within the church.

I come from a tradition of congregational church government where absolute congregational autonomy is stressed at both a theoretical and theological level. In such a system you would think that a person would be free to express opinions on Scripture contrary to the view of the group. This is not always true. Dissenters are often silenced or expelled from the group. Some even change their views and conform to social norms for Scripture interpretations.

Studies on the behavior of groups towards people with deviant positions reveal what happens in theological circles. The study of Schacter investigated pressure towards conformity in a group. The various groups in the study included three confederates, 1) a *deviant* who consistently advocated a position opposite to that of the group norm, 2) a *slider* who at first deviated from the group but then changed his or her mind, and 3) a "no-mode" person who adopted the model opinion of the group. The group directed a lot of energy towards the slider and the deviant. Eventually the deviant was excluded from the group processes.[4]

Robert Douglas illustrates how individuals have been pressured to conform to an interpretative view of a denomination. He documents the fact that during the 1960s the unofficial hierarchy within the Church of Christ sought to silence persons who expressed contrary views on social issues, such as civil rights. In an ecclesiastical system that espouses a congregational form of government, Douglas points out that:

1. There is an unofficial extracongregational hierarchy of prestigious preachers, editors, and college administrators who shape opinion and interpretation of

Scripture within the system. Similar "old-boy net-works" or informal power structures are evident throughout the fabric of other church systems.

2. The opinion of this unofficial hierarchy prevailed in areas of social commentary. Their views on social issues reflected a right-wing, political doctrine rather than an honest scriptural exegesis.

3. The contribution of this power system was to facilitate "doctrinal cohesion, social pronouncement and the expression of a definite sense of denominational identity and worth."[5]

Certain dissenters within the Church of Christ system sought to demonstrate the validity of some of the political aspirations of civil rights leaders such as Martin Luther King, Jr. Scriptural passages such as "there is neither Jew nor Greek, slave nor free, male nor female" (Gal 3:28) were brought to bear on issues of freedom and justice. The censure by the unofficial hierarchy was sometimes swift and harsh, other times subtle and insidious. The dissenters were denied the denominational forum, including pulpit and journal, for their views. Some of the persons within the hierarchy agreed privately with the dissenters but publicly took a stand against them. The above is a patent illustration of how the needs and politics of a group help shape the interpretation of Scripture.

The illustration of the Church of Christ by Douglas is not unique to the history of the wider church. In August 1979 Stanley Gundry was asked to resign from the faculty of Moody Bible Institute over the interpretive issue of women in the home, church, and society. Gundry and his wife Patricia espoused a non-traditional interpretation of the biblical data. Their viewpoint and Patricia's writing and speaking activities proved to be politically sensitive even though they were not in conflict with the Institute's doctrinal statement or official policy. Since the Gundrys would not conform their interpretation of particular Scripture passages to the unofficial traditional view of some administrators and constituents, the Institute tried to reduce dissonance within the system by asking Stanley to leave Moody. Dissenters within a group create a state of cognitive imbalance. The leaders can reduce the dissonance by silencing or discrediting dissenters.

THE NEEDS OF THE GROUP

One of the objectives of the modern ecumenical movement is the uniting of various church groups. The movement seeks to reconcile churches with different doctrinal statements, which are based on the interpretations of Scripture. While it is true that churches have split over important doctrinal issues, social forces have also operated in the formation of denominations. H. Richard Niebuhr in *The Social Sources of Denominationalism* comments:

> Advancing and defending their positions on the basis of proof-texts drawn from the Scriptures, it has been possible for various sects to take anti-thetical views of the Christian or unChristian character of these institutions. Only the purest novice in history will seek the explanation of such opinions in the proof-texts from which they purport to derive.[6]

The author goes on to demonstrate how the various denominations and sects have arisen out of the social conditions of their day rather than from a biblical interpretation problem reason. "The spirit and doctrines of Lutheranism derive not only from the New Testament but also from Luther's German temperament and from the political conditions of the church in Germany."[7] Sometimes the church is a reflection of the caste system of society. At all times the church reflects the economic, policital, social, and personal aspirations of its people. Many times the Bible is adapted to these multifaceted human needs. The disinherited gravitate toward an apocalyptic emphasis and the oppressed adopt a theology that supports their elitism.

Cultural myopia in the interpretation of Scripture can be seen on a national scale. Some Dutch Reformed theologians in South Africa interpret the sphere sovereignty of Kuyperian Calvinism as the basis for the socio-political superstructure of apartheid. The separation of the races is seen as God-ordained so that, in their view, the Bible supports apartheid. John de Gruchy in *The Church Struggle in South Africa* writes:

> Kuyper's idea of separate spheres of sovereignty embedded in creation corresponded well with the Lutheran doctrine of the 'orders of creation' as expounded by German missionary . . . Dutch Reformed Church policy. Together they have had considerable influence on South African social history. Indeed, it helps explain why at a later date the DRC could give its support to the Nationalist policy of separate development as being in accord with the will of God. It was this theological position which provided the religious ground for the policy.[8]

The preservation of the nationhood of a white minority in the face of a perceived black threat (swart gevaar) may well be the basis for such a misuse of Scripture. This is yet another incident of need defining interpretation.

David Myers quotes a series of social psychology experiments that indicate how we cling tenaciously to beliefs even when they are disconfirmed. The studies have to do with planting a falsehood in people's minds and then attempting to discredit the belief. Myers writes:

> In each experiment, first a belief was established, either by proclaiming it true or else by inducing the person to conclude its truth after inspecting two sample cases; then, people were asked to explain *why* it was true; and finally the initial information was totally discredited—the person was told the truth, that the information was manufactured for the experiment and that half of the people in the experiment were given opposing theory or data. Nevertheless, amazingly, the new belief typically survived the discrediting about 75% intact, presumably because the person still retained the invented explanation for the belief.[9]

Why is it that in the face of nonconforming evidence we cling to a belief? There are three possible explanations:

1. The belief gives us our unique identity.
2. Our ancestors have expended sweat, blood, and tears for a particular position. To give up the belief would be like telling a group of Marines who had just captured an enemy position that their effort was a waste of time.
3. Our identification with a particular social class compels us to remain committed to a theological position, e.g., Presbyterian doctrine for upper middle-class whites.

Furthermore, we so value the approval of our group that we change in the midst of conflicting cognitions towards the opinion of the group even if we are still dissenters in the privacy of our hearts. While there are social pressures around the person that create the need for mental gymnastics in the support of a particular biblical position there are even larger arenas to consider. The next section will explore the impact of culture on interpretation.

THE CULTURE GAP

There is a wide gulf between the culture of the biblical author and the culture in which the modern-day interpreter lives. The chief requisites for good interpretation are the cultural assumptions of the particular scriptural passage, and the assumptions of the interpreter's culture regarding the issue or subject in view.

Sometimes identifying culture-bound interpretations or reflexive applications is difficult. Despite Lindsell's thesis that the plain view of Scripture is there for all to see, Kraft calls for cultural sensitivity when he writes: "Those unaware of the pervasive influence of their own culture on their interpretations often slip unconsciously into the assumption that arriving at most supracultural truth is simply a matter of accepting the 'clear' or plain 'meanings' of Scripture."[10]

Kraft has a point when he alerts interpreters to the cultural gap between the interpreter and author of Scripture. However, he has been severely criticized by Carl Henry and others for grossly underestimating the clarity and objectivity of much of Scripture apart from cultural influence. Henry writes:

> Not only does he grossly understate the amount of objective doctrinal and ethical teaching that the Bible conveys in specific situations, but the very passages he acknowledges as such contradict the notion that divine truth is to be reformulated in divergent cultural specifications as an internal response.[11]

Kraft agrees that there is supracultural truth in Scripture, but he is not very clear or extensive in his exposition of such truth. However, he is right in emphasizing that the Bible is a multicultural book with distance between Hebrew and European cultures. The science of hermeneutics—utilizing the best tools of disciplines such as archaeology and linguistics—has assured us of relatively good access to the understanding of the meaning of Scripture.

Morris, in a realistic evaluation of sociocultural influences on hermeneutics, writes, "Culture is not a windowless room. It is possible to see beyond one's own culture and enter imaginatively into that of someone else."[12] The best tools of hermeneutics enable us to open these windows. We can discover the congruence of meanings between words and passages in two languages. Charles Taber is right when he warns us of the cultural gap. He illustrates the point with reference to *father* in Scripture. He writes:

> Even as apparently universal a category as *father* (of obvious importance to theology for its metaphoric use in reference to God) turns out to have quite diverse meanings depending on a number of factors: is the society bilineal like ours, patrilineal like those of Bible times, or matrilineal like a number of contemporary societies? Is the father regarded as a remote, forbidding authority figure, or is he close and indulgent? Is the adult male authority figure for a child his biological father, or his mother's brother? And so on.[13]

The "clear" meaning of Scripture is therefore only discerned, in the case of the use of *father,* when the cultural gap is bridged.

I am more concerned here with the contribution of

81

the interpreter's culture to different governing assumptions. The Scriptures *are* authoritative and inspired, but extra-Scriptural perspectives (e.g., covenant theology, dispensational theology) do not share the same authority of the meaning as that inherent in the Bible. Each position represents the effort of a culture-bound group of theologians attempting to grasp the meaning of Scripture through the construction of models.

Having a culture free context in which to hear the word of God would be impossible, of course. The Bible is like a shaft of light that penetrates the mist of our culture-boundedness. We are reminded again and again by missiologists such as Kraft that culture is not something necessarily right or wrong and that God speaks through culture. After all, the Word of God became flesh. The boundedness of that flesh was His Jewishness. His acts and words would not have been intelligible to a bushman in Africa. They would not have understood all His Jewish illustrations, habits, and actions. Yet because of His essential humanness He speaks to all cultures. The Son of Man speaks to all people. The need for a personal relationship with God, the redemptive act on the Cross, and His risen presence is a timely word to all people, especially when presented in their cultural terms, e.g., the "Peace Child" message so ably given by Richardson.[14] He demonstrated that there are possibilities of a redemptive analogy within even the most 'pagan' cultures. Such analogies can be used as a point of contact with a people when the Christian communicates the gospel with them.

Each culture has its own readily available folklore, legends, and myths that can be related to the gospel message. Theological blueprints and models can be formulated and tested within the context of the language and culture domain of a particular people. Each model is useful to the extent that it is in concert with the essential message of the Scriptures. Ultimately the Scriptures themselves are the standard of orthodoxy. The Word of God asks its own questions and gives its own answers. The Word is never irrelevant to the questions of faith and life asked by each culture. Culture is, however, the stage on which these questions are asked.

CULTURALLY EVOKED HERMENEUTICS

Cultural conditions sometimes shape the receptivity of a people towards a particular hermeneutical position. In many third world contexts the receptivity of the church to "liberation-theology" is abused on a keen awareness of the gap between the "have" and "have-not" nations. The philosophical roots of liberation theology are definitely Hegelian with the view that God is not transcendent over His world "but revealing Himself through the secular experience of the process of change in human history.[15] The seminal thinkers in liberation theology are, more specifically, the young Hegelians. They present a theology that, according to Hamilton, "takes both its basic premise (the oppression/liberation polarity) and its basic strategy (the belief that salvation can come only through the revolutionary action of the oppressed)."[16]

No wonder then that persons living in the midst of oppressive regimes and structures respond well to a hermeneutical system that identifies salvation as a liberation or permanent cultural revolution. Marxism is easily wedded with such a theology, and intellectuals and politically astute leaders use theology to exploit the just grievances of the downtrodden. Such a marriage is easily understood when the message of Christianity has not always spoken to unjust structures in the third world. The socio-economic and political conditions of oppressed people, plus an unbiblical Hegelian philosophy, become the interpretive norm for the meaning of Scripture. Hermeneutics is shaped by orthopracy (the practical application of beliefs) rather than orthodoxy (right thinking). Thiselton comments that the preunderstanding of certain liberation theologians is shaped by praxis. They claim that theoretical knowledge, "especially the philosophical values associated with the Western bourgeoisie, distort the message of the Bible and obscure the rights of the text. There is no such thing as purely neutral knowledge."[17] We all have culturally conditioned lenses through which we interpret our world. Such conscious bias, according to Thiselton, "sharpens the problem of objectivity in biblical hermeneutics. A mere awareness of the problem of preunderstanding is not enough to solve the problems to which this phenomenon gives rise."[18]

Liberation theology is not the only example of a culturally-evoked hermeneutic. The current debate on the role of women in the church and home reflects a response to secular feminism. The consciousness of the church was raised and there was a strong response on some fronts resulting in a reaction against a male chauvinistic hierarchy. Seeing that salvation can be identified with liberation when a woman begins with a concrete experience of oppression is not difficult. The pain is so great, the church is sometimes insensitive, and the new interpretative system is a viable alternative for the oppressive situation. We cannot allow the culturally conditioned and topical significance of a passage to alter the meaning of Scripture. The flow of interpretation is from meaning to significance and not vice versa. The only way we can get any interpretation to transcend its cultural-rootedness is to test again and again for the meaning. The Divinely inspired text has a life of its own that *can* speak to all forms of oppression and cultural rootedness.

SOCIO-POLITICAL ISSUES

A key question then is, "Do we allow social conditions and theological issues to be the *determining* factor in our hermeneutics?" Such a preunderstanding would militate against letting the Scripture speak for itself. The question should rather be, "Will we allow social and theological issues to challenge *our* bourgeois and biased interpretations and drive us back to the meaning of the Word?" The social conditions in the third world and other places, the indefensible consumptive practices in North America, and the poor and oppressed individuals and systems should call us to a radical discipleship where the characteristic mode is the servant and not the master. We not only need to be aware of our own culturally determined preunderstanding but also allow the crucial questions of the day to enable us to hear the meaning of the Scripture in a new light.

The history of theology is replete with examples of issues impacting theologizing. Such an impact of culture on theology can lead to cultural reductionism. For instance, liberation theologians believe in a liberation hermeneutic *because* it furthers their economic interests in Latin America; equalitarian theologians reject hierarchy and accept an equilitarian hermeneutic *because* it works for the cause of the Equal Rights Amendment. No matter how just our cause, we cannot allow the cause to control the system of biblical interpretation. We must let the cause direct us to search for a scriptural answer, but ultimately the Scripture must be allowed to give its own message.

The same thing may be said for the language of culture. For instance, the language of psychology has become a part of the language of our age. Much of the "psychobabble" today is about as useful as a bumper sticker statement in providing a comprehensive answer

85

to the issues of life. Terms such as *ego states, life scripts, unconscious motives,* and *repressed anger* are often vaguely defined and used. Explaining biblical passages with the use of such terms is not helpful. To say that Jesus was acting out of the "adult"—a term from Transactional Analysis—when he cleansed the temple hardly describes the meaning of the scriptural passage. We can only use the language of culture for the language of Scripture if they both have the same meaning. Although my psychology impacts the type of questions I ask of the Bible, I dare not psychologize the meaning of Scripture.

Each age has its key issues. The spirit of the times (*Zeitgeist*) shapes many things from the awarding of the Nobel Peace Prize to the ideologies of the day such as liberation theology. Emphasis on various doctrinal issues rises and falls with this *Zeitgeist.*

Some writers, for example Stanly N. Gundry, question whether the determining factor in the history of eschatology has been Scripture itself or the *Zeitgeist.* Gundry writes, "We are still faced with the phenomenon of the correlation between changing currents within Christian eschatologies and the vicissitudes of the times generally."[19] He points to the rise of *amillennialism* in A.D. 400 with St. Augustine. The spirit of the times was positive, the Constantinian era provided legal status for the church, the suffering of the downtrodden was alleviated, and it seemed that God was ruling in the *now.* The millennial kingdom had come. The lion was lying down with the lamb. Regarding the rise of *postmillennialism,* the optimistic view of the Puritans in the seventeenth century could have been the formative factor in this system of interpretation. Gundry writes:

> But I would also like to tentatively suggest that
> it parallels and perhaps is a theological reflection
> of the optimistic views of mankind's potential

and opportunities with an expanding geo-
graphical horizon and an ever-growing
confidence in the powers of man's reason. Be
that as it may, it is significant that in England
the preaching of the 'latter-day glory,' the
postmillennial vision, reached its height in the
late 1640s, and then it had a precipitous de-
cline.[20]

Gundry is, however, not presenting a reductionistic
view that claims that an eschatology is the result of *only*
socio-political climates of their day. There are other issues within Evangelicalism that should not be knee-jerk
reactions to the question of the day. The opinions and
issues of the day certainly need to speak to the thinking
of the Christian, but our convictions should not be
shaped only by our social milieu, but also by the divine
revelation of the Word.

CULTURE-BOUND TRANSLATION

Certain questions emerge as one considers the task
of biblical translation. Is there such a thing as a translation free of cultural distortion? Even if the translator
understands the cultural world of the Bible, as well as
that of the people who read the translation, is the product undistorted by cultural values or norms? Kraft sets
forth some useful principles whereby a person can produce a translation "faithful both to the original author
and message and to the intended impact that the message was to have upon the original readers."[21] He
recognizes such a translation as a *dynamic-equivalent*
process. It does not involve a one-to-one correspondence between the words of the author and those of the
receptor language. Forms differ from culture to culture.
The word *flesh* (Greek, *sarx*) means one thing to a first-
century Christian in a Graeco-Roman culture and
another thing to an Australian Aborigine. A good

translator, according to Kraft, will rewrite "the material in the appropriate style (forms) of the receptor language to produce a dynamically equivalent effect on the hearers."[22] The primary focus, then, is on the receptor with the intent of preserving the divine message of the original text.

Great care should be taken not to accommodate to the issues of the day in the process of translation. In an article in *Christianity Today,* A. and B. Mickelsen point to numerous instances where translators of the Bible demonstrated sexism in translation.[23] While the Mickelsens' point out much valid sexism in translation, they also seem to argue that the word *head* means only "source." In fact, there are alternative meanings that include "authority." An equalitarian value system must not be allowed to dictate how a word should be translated. Equalitarian values can challenge blatant sexism in the church but cannot be allowed to distort the actual meaning of Scripture. The text and context of Scripture must be allowed to stand alone and to speak for itself. We should attempt to be as accurate as possible in determining the meaning of the text.

CONCLUSION

In chapters 2 and 3 a survey was made of the impact of personality and society on the interpretation of the Bible. Many traditional readings of Scripture can be distorted because of the personal and social influences on interpretation. The behavioral sciences tell us a great deal about the strengths of human nature. A better understanding of the personal and cultural lenses through which we view the Bible helps us better discern its God-given meaning.

In order to get a valid reading on the interpretation of Scripture we have to diligently pursue the God-given and unchanging meaning. This *meaning* is derived from the process of exegesis and synthesis of the text of Scripture. Its *application* or significance varies from age to age and issue to issue. The text has a life of its own that can, in my opinion, transcend the intentions and meaning of its human author.

Cultural, social, and personality influences have their greatest impact on the meaning of the text at the points of synthesis and application. Here the person is attempting an association between parts and the whole as well as the text to the current human situation. Here again we rely on the organic unity of the Bible. The divine Word does not contradict itself. It is the human factor that brings about the confusion in interpretation.

NOTES

[1]Gordon Allport, "The Historical Background of Modern Psychology," in G. Lindzey and E. Aronson, eds., *The Handbook of Social Psychology.* (Reading, Mass.: Addison-Wesley, 1968), p. 3.

[2]David Myers, *The Inflated Self* (New York: Seabury, 1980), p. 53.

[3]G. C. Berkouwer, *Studies in Dogmatics: Holy Scripture* (Grand Rapids: Eerdmans, 1979), p. 115.

[4]S. Schacter, *The Psychology of Affiliation* (Palo Alto, Calif.: Stanford University Press, 1959).

[5]Robert Douglas, "Power, Its Locus and Function in Defining Social Commentary in the Church of Christ," Unpublished doctoral dissertation, University of Southern California, 1980, p. 353.

[6]H. Richard Niebuhr, *The Social Sources of Denominationalism* (Cleveland: World, 1929), p. 14.

[7]Ibid., p. 16.

[8]John de Gruchy, *The Church Struggle in South Africa* (Cape Town: David Philip, 1979), p. 10.

[9]Myers, *The Inflated Self,* p. 57.

[10]Charles Kraft, *Christianity in Culture* (New York: Orbis Books, 1979), p. 131.

[11]C. Henry, "The Cultural Relativizing of Revelation." *Trinity Journal,* Fall 1980, p. 156.

[12]Leon Moins, "The Culture Gap," *Christianity Today,* June 1978, p. 49.

[13]Charles Taber, "Is There More than One Way to do Theology?" *Gospel in Context,* Jan. 1978, p. 8.

[14]D. Richardson, *Peace Child* (Glendale, Calif.: Regal, 1974).

[15]Kenneth Hamilton, "Liberation Theology, Lessons Positive and Negative," in *Evangelicals and Liberation.* Edited by Carl E. Armerding

(Nutley, N.J.: Presbyterian and Reformed, 1977), p. 3.

[16]Ibid., p. 5.

[17]A. T. Thiselton, *The Two Horizons: New Testament Hermeneutics and Philosophical Description* (Grand Rapids: Eerdmans, 1980), p. 111.

[18]Ibid., p. 113.

[19]Stanley N. Gundry, "Hermeneutics or *Zeitgeist* as the Determining Factor in the History of Eschatologies." *Journal of the Evangelical Theological Society,* 1977, *20* (1), p. 55.

[20]Ibid., p. 51.

[21]Kraft, *Christianity in Culture,* p. 271.

[22]Ibid., p. 275.

[23]A. and B. Mickelsen, "Does Male Domination Tarnish our Translations?" *Christianity Today,* October 1979, pp. 23–29.

A Psychological Hermeneutic—
Insight and Responsibility

4

Very few people in evangelical Christianity consciously and willfully twist the meaning and application of the Bible. A good scholar aims at maximum validity in hermeneutics. The goal is to reflect the true position of the divine and human authors of Scripture. The fact that we have mutually exclusive explanations for the meaning and application of some parts of the Bible suggests that we have not heard the last word on the "true" position, however. The differences among biblical interpreters are not just to be accounted for by inadequate methods of interpretation. The current science of hermeneutics has come a long way in refining these methods. The reason for different interpretations may be found in a place other than inadequate technique. It may be due to the fact that we are reluctant to *revise* or *change* our theological models. Personality, society, and culture act as lenses through which the Bible is viewed.

Previous chapters have spelled out some of these influencing factors. What, then, do we do with our fear of revision and change? How can we compensate for personal and social bias? My thesis is that the fear of the opinion of others causes interpreters to freeze in their tracks on the journey to better interpretation. We need to hear the Divine call to courage, understand the nature and manifestation of our fears, and utilize the resources of the church to give us insight to ourselves and the Bible. However, insight to fear is not an end in itself. The goal is responsible action that results in accurate interpretation of the Word of Truth. It is only when we cease to be imprisoned by our fears that we can be true artists and scientists who hear and obey the meaning of the Bible.

THE CALL TO COURAGE

The fear of the opinion of others inhibits the expression of creative interpretations, the examination of theological blueprints, and the change of interpretative systems. We do well to heed the counsel of Kahil Gibran who writes:

> My soul preached to me and said,
> 'Do not be delighted because of
> praise, and do not be distressed
> because of blame.'

> Ere my soul counselled me, I
> doubted the worth of my work.
> Now I realize that the trees blossom
> in spring and bear fruit in summer
> without seeking praise; and they drop
> their leaves in autumn and become naked
> in winter without fearing blame. [1]

A heavy personal investment in the good opinion of others can cause people to misinterpret the Scriptures. It is possible for an interpreter to be always looking over his or her shoulder to determine the opinion of the church. We sometimes fear its censure as we expand or revise theological models dear to the church. The brave souls who dare to challenge the theological tenets of the church may suffer ostracism for their interpretative insights. Some have been relieved of church appointments because they questioned basic traditions of the church. Other theologians may be less explicit in their opposition to interpretative conclusions because they have signed a contract to teach at a seminary even though they disagree with some of the methods of interpretation in the institution.

We dare not sit in judgment on each other. Only the Lord can judge the motives of the heart. He calls us away from fear. An example of such a call was seen in the prophet Jeremiah. He was commissioned to speak on behalf of the Lord but presented a series of fearful excuses. The Lord responded again and again telling Jeremiah not to be afraid:

> Do not say, "I am only a child." You must go to everyone I send you to and say whatever I command you. Do not be afraid of them, for I am with you and will rescue you. . . . Get yourself ready! Stand up and say to them whatever I command you. Do not be terrified by them, or I will terrify you before them (Jer. 1:7–8, 17).

Like Jeremiah, we need to hear the call to courage in the declaration of the meaning and application of the Word. We need to understand *why* we are afraid of the people and then decide how to behave in appropriate and loving ways towards them. We steel ourselves with a courage that comes from the Lord and seek to gain insight to the origins of fear.

The Nature of Fear

Fear is the very stuff of both growth and stagnation. Psychologist Otto Rank (1884–1939) developed the notion that each person lives in a polarity of tension between the fear of life and the fear of death. The terms *life* and *death* are used in a unique fashion. In the fear of death, the person dreads union, fusion, or dependency. He or she needs to assert uniqueness before God and the world, and fears the loss of such freedom. On the other hand, the fear of life is found in one who dreads the possibility of separation and individualization. The whole of life is expressed on the stage of fear.

The early experience of fear is found in the child eighteen to twenty-four months old who seeks to venture from its mother in order to experience the world. To remain forever in a symbiotic relationship with mother means emotional death. The child needs to develop its own ego boundaries, explore the world, and develop its own experimental powers. It is a life or death struggle.

The polarity of fear in the human journey was also described by Sören Kierkegaard, who developed the notion that all humans struggle with their possibility and necessity. Possibility represents all that we can be and is fully realized in relationship to God. Necessity represents our humanity, mortality, and frailty. Ernest Becker, in an original and profound exposition of Kierkegaard, points to the fact that for those whose life has too much possibility and who deny necessity end up in psychosis. He writes:

> Too much possibility is the attempt by the person to overvalue the powers of the symbolic self. It reflects the attempt to exaggerate one half of the human dualism at the expense of the other. In this sense, what we call schizophrenia is an attempt by the symbolic self to deny the limitations of the finite body; in doing so, the entire person is pulled off balance and de-

stroyed. It is as though the freedom of creativity that stems from within the symbolic self
cannot be contained by the body, and the person is torn apart.[2]

The other side of the human spectrum, the repres-
sion or denial of possibility, represents the person who
focuses too much on human limitations. Becker commenting on the fearfulness associated with depression,
writes:

> Depressive psychosis is the extreme on the con-
> tinuum of *too much necessity,* that is, too much
> finitude, too much limitation by the body and
> the behaviors of the person in the real world,
> and not enough freedom of the inner self, of
> inner symbolic possibility. This is how we
> understand depressive psychosis today: as a
> bogging down in the demands of others—
> family, job, the narrow horizon of daily
> duties.[3]

There are no easy ways to health in the midst of
such a polarity of fears. The journey into health is by
means of insight into one's humanity with its limitations
and potential.

The Manifestations of Fear

Biblical interpreters need to understand their fears if
they are to determine the meaning and application of the
Bible. What then does the fear of too much necessity or
too much possibility have to do with the process of
biblical interpretation? The answer is encapsulated in
two words, dependence and independence. Both positions represent an unhealthy and fearful relationship
between the believer and the church. The independent
person is unheeding of any need or opinion but his own.
Such a person tramples the church and other believers in

the drive to establish his or her own way. A dependent person, on the other hand, is too much bogged down in the opinion of peers. He or she learns to be a helpless victim that needs the neurotic approval of the church.

An example of dependence can be seen in an enmeshment of identity between the person and the church. It has some similarities to the unhealthy parent/child relationship where the adult needs the infant to validate his or her being. The resulting attitude is "I do not want this child to assert its own will and become a separate being; I want to keep the child close to love me and meet my needs." A parent with such a posture towards the child is threatened by an act of independence on the part of the child. As the child grows it is often torn between meeting the neurotic needs of the parent and asserting its own person. Such an emotional impasse is seen in the case of the church that says to those dependent persons, "You can pastor my church, serve as an elder, or teach on my faculty, if you interpret the Bible in such a manner." Such a person may be seeking the church's validation for personhood. Personal wishes, and often growth, are put aside for fear of the censure by the church. Such a symbiosis is represented in the words

> We do our thing together
> I am here to meet all your needs and expectations
> And you are here to meet mine
> We had to meet, and it was beautiful
> I can't imagine it turning out any other way.[4]

The independent interpreter operates from fear as well. He or she manifests the unhealthy reaction seen in some adolescents who say

> I do my thing, and you do your thing

I am not in this world to live up to your expec-
tations
And you are not here in this world to live up to
mine
You are you and I am I
And if by chance we meet, it's beautiful
If not, it can't be helped.[5]

Both positions, dependence and independence, are unhealthy and force the person into a posture of fear in
relationship to the church.

THE CHURCH—THE CONTEXT
FOR COURAGE

There is another, more healthy, way. It is the way
of interdependence. It is the place of mutual submission.
No person is a law unto himself or herself. Mutual accountability in interpretative issues should act as a check
and balance but not restrain independent and creative
thought. "Submit yourselves one to another" (Eph.
5:21); this is not a command but a call for a voluntary
servant spirit that seeks the best interests of the other.
And so it should be between the believer and the church,
where creativity of interpretation lives in the context of
love and responsibility. It is the way of cooperation and
courage. Such interdependence is the realization of the
ideal of biblical "body life." The theory of cooperation
is presented here. Later, the practical application will be
spelled out.

The science of hermeneutics with its significant
personal elements, such as creativity and theory testing,
dare not become a *private* venture. The worldwide and
historical community of believers is involved in the
validation of each personal quest for the meaning of the
Scriptures. Karl Barth expressed a strong belief that theology or dogmatics should be the task of the whole
church. He warns:

> The man who seeks to occupy himself with
> dogmatics and deliberately puts himself outside
> the Church would have to reckon with the fact
> that for him the object of dogmatics would be a
> lie, and should not be surprised if after the first
> steps he could not find his bearings, or even did
> damage.[6]

The person and mother church must have the courage to change schemas and shift paradigms as they approach Scripture. But, we must not work alone. Theology, as an interpretative discipline, is a dynamic process. Dogma is not fixed for all time. The only goals are the quest for the meaning of the Word and the freedom of individuals to hear the Word for themselves. This is not the easy way. Seminaries and churches change their statements of faith with new interpretative insight. Constituencies and financial supporters react and withdraw support. Which way will the new interpretative insight take us? We need each other in the quest for better interpretation. The watchword of the interdependent interpreter is expressed by Kahil Gibran:

> Sing and dance together and be joyous,
> but let each one of you be alone
> Even as the strings of a lute are alone
> though they quiver with the same music
> And stand together yet not too near together;
> For the pillars of the temple stand apart,
> and the oak tree and the cypress grow
> not in each other's shadow
> But let there be spaces in your togetherness
> And let the winds of the heavens dance between
> you.[7]

There is a great personal, cultural, historically conditioned diversity within evangelical Christianity today. It is in the community of believers that we translate the "truth of previous ages into contemporary expression."[8] We listen attentively to a whole spectrum of theological thought. We sit at the feet of instructors like Kierkegaard, Calvin, Augustine, and Barth and let them form our theological paradigms. Hermeneutics is not an "ex nihilo" phenomenon. The fact that the meaning and application of Scripture has been discerned by countless persons throughout the history of the church should cause us to hesitate before we change or modify our theological theories. We can refurbish the structure of orthodox theology but we must be very careful about removing its cornerstones. We must hesitate and be cautious about tampering with the faith once delivered to the saints. We also must recognize that while there is room for creativity, it must not be outside the context of the unity of revelation. We cannot formulate models that abandon the givenness of the meaning of Scripture.

Where do we go in our interpretative enterprise when we have identified our fears and declared the church to be the context for courage? The labeling of the problem is not the magic solution. Action must follow insight. The truth about myself does not set me free, but an obedient response to the One who is the Truth does set me free. Furthermore, a dynamic relationship with Christ requires that I practice the truth. In the words of the apostle James, "Anyone, then, who knows the good he ought to do and doesn't do it, sins" (James 4:17). Psychologist Sheldon Kopp expresses a similar thought as he reflects on his own therapy. He writes that after intellectualizing his problems he stubbornly insisted that the unexamined life was not worth living. We might be inclined to ignore the reciprocal fact that the unlived life is not worth examining. Insight may come as a great "aha" to some readers, but we cannot end the book with insight alone. Responsible action must be our response to any new awareness of our personal biases.

THE CALL FOR RESPONSIBILITY

It is imperative that responsible action follow hard on the heels of the insight to our fears. What are our personal and corporate responsibilities when we become aware of bias in biblical interpretation? What do we do after the prophet has broken through our rationalizations and said, "Thou art the man"? Do we allow such pearls of wisdom to be cast before the swine? The suggested responses to insight in the following pages fit with the presuppositions of a psychologist. There are other solutions suggested in books on hermeneutics. There may be overlap, but these are offered from the point of view of the behavior sciences. We must start with the authority of the Bible.

The Bible Regulates its Own Interpretation

Charles Taber after an excellent treatise on the need for multi-cultural input to the determination of meaning in Scripture, writes: "All theologies, western or non-western, must be continually brought into subjection to the inspired Scriptures, responsibly interpreted."[9] When we approach the Word it tells us of its own authority and profitability. "All Scripture is God-breathed and is useful for teaching, rebuking, correcting and training in righteousness" (2 Tim. 3:16).

We cannot doubt that the Bible speaks for itself on matters of faith and practice. The Word became flesh and lived among us. He defined Himself for us. Some of His words and acts were beyond the grasp of His hearers. Sometimes the seed fell into fruitful ground. The seed has its own life. The Word has its own cognitive content. The Spirit of God assists in the communication of His Word. I realize that the last few statements are more of an affirmation of faith on my part, but my beliefs are grounded on my view of the authority of Scripture. It is not an authority that I have given the Word but one that the Word gives itself. I, therefore, lean towards the Reformers' view of "perspicuity," in which the Scriptures are sufficiently clear in matters of faith and practice. However, we do not have an exhaustive understanding of the meaning of Scripture because of our human limitations and preunderstandings. We sometimes see through a glass, darkly. The understanding of culture, psychology, and all that goes into the science and art of hermeneutics helps clear away the smog of confusion. Like people in cities with smog problems, we try to see despite the smog. Interpreters must get rid of the smog and see clearly the Word of God again. The perspective of the interpreter imparts both the distortion as well as the discovery of meaning. We also need to recognize that the Word of God has shaped whole cultures, altered nations, permeated legal and ethical systems, and changed lives. While our human preunderstanding acts as a lens through which we see the meaning of Scripture, the reverse is also true—meaning shapes our preunderstanding and the resultant theoretical, political, and cultural systems.

The Bible is therefore its own starting point and final authority on its interpretation. It has a life and unity of its own that binds all the parts together. For long ages, theologians have sought for the unifying principle in Scripture. For some it is the theme of salvation, for others it is the concept of covenant. All these theories of unity are subject to the scrutiny of the artist and the scientist.

The Artist and Scientist Cooperate

The second way we exercise responsibility in biblical interpretation is through the cooperation of the artist with the scientist. William James pointed to the unacknowledged role of temperament in the history and practice of philosophy; he used the terms "tough-minded" and "tender-minded" with reference to philosophy. This is the hybrid that I think is the best interpreter of Scripture: the artist/scientist. I have already expounded on the scientist component with its emphasis on validity, theory building, and testing. I also alluded to the fact that true science cannot ignore the personal element.[10]

The artist aspect of the interpreter places great emphasis on creativity and personal involvement with the text. I reiterate that creativity is not an "ex-nihilo" process. We do not create truth from nothing in the same sense that God created the world. Creativity is used in a specialized sense and has the connotation of ideational fluency. The process is part of the God-given ability to think divergently, to formulate new models, to take the data of Scripture and find the meaning of the part as it relates to the whole. The process proceeds with the fear of the Lord but also with boldness in the face of people who would disagree. The fear of the Lord is the beginning of wisdom. The fear of people is the end of creativity.

The artist is not just concerned with the text but also with his or her own person. There needs to be a high level of self-awareness in theological enterprise. I am not saying that theology is nothing but self-reflection. Such subjective reductionism detracts from the Word that has a meaning in itself. The person, however, must not exclude self-discovery from the task of theologizing. The true artist/scientist asks the searching questions posed by James Woelfel, who writes:

> What are the main theological themes with
> which I have been preoccupied? What elements
> in my own life-history may have played a role

in choosing to emphasize those themes and not others? Who are my theological 'heroes'? What is it I admire about them—their themes, their methods, their style, their *persona,* their life-experience? Why do they strike responsive chords in myself? Who are my theological 'villains', and why? Why do I simply tend to ignore some thinkers and movements that are obviously worthy of attention. What are the elements of rationalization in the reasons I give for my theological likes, dislikes, and indifferences?[11]

An honest response to such questions will help the interpreter get past personal bias and use the mind creatively. Sometimes, however, personal bias militates against the discovery of meaning. Here the artist must respond to the suggestion of the ancient sage, "Know thyself." The artist must seek personal insight through all the means available in the Christian community.

Therapeutic Resources in the Church

At this point the biblical scholar, or interpreter of scripture, may react and say, Is this psychologist suggesting that I need a psychotherapist?

If we see psychotherapy only as a procedure used to heal crazy people, we have a somewhat myopic understanding of the process. Our stereotypes of the mental health profession may come from extremes like those represented in the film "One Flew Over the Cuckoo's Nest." We need to hear such recent statements of psychotherapy as those presented by Christian psychologists.[12] I do not intend to duplicate these, but consideration should be given to the idea that a therapist may help an interpreter understand and change personal and cultural biases. Psychotherapy is one of the practical applications by which the behavioral sciences alleviate human suffering and promote personal growth.

The nature of psychotherapy that could help an interpreter depends on the theoretical orientation of the therapist, and there are various psychotherapies used by Christian mental health practitioners. However, no matter what the therapist's theoretical orientation, the context should be one that produces understanding and change. The ideal context involves factors such as empathy, the generation of hope, the practicing of new and healthful behaviors and attitudes, and a warm, personal relationship with the therapist. In such a context the biblical interpreter may explore the whole range of biases mentioned in this book including:

- transference relationship toward authority figures or symbols, for example, unconscious compliance with or rebellion against the church's interpretation.
- insecurity in an ambiguous situation, for example, the need for a final statement on a particular doctrine or practice.
- selective attention toward an interpretation that is politically and/or socially expedient.

The desired goal would be the elimination of personal bias. The soul-searching allows an interpreter to enter new possibilities of understanding. The quest for personal insight needs an environment where fear is minimized and acceptance and freedom are predominant.

An Environment of Acceptance

Through the years I have discovered, much to my chagrin, that I have often been very unaccepting toward others. For instance, there are elements in the moral majority that I find repugnant. In a sense I agree with the bumper sticker that says, "The Moral Majority—is

Neither!" Strong feelings and convictions toward an opposing position cannot be eliminated. Jesus hardly adopted a 'milquetoast' attitude towards the merchants in the temple. The problem with strong feelings is unacceptance of the person. I need to listen to the Moral Majority and reexamine my position on abortion and obscenity. I need to grant others the freedom to state a biblical position and not be threatened and react as if my life were at stake. I need to accept others as persons with value. There are many places in evangelical Christianity where it seems that a commitment to an interpretative position is an issue of life and death. If an individual questions or departs from the interpretative framework there is a knee-jerk reaction of unacceptance or rejection by the constituency. I have surveyed some of the personal and social reasons for such inflexibility and I feel that the time has come for acceptance without surrendering the use of the Word of God as a plumbline for orthodoxy.

What is this climate of acceptance? I find in my reflections on personal growth that a very destructive attitude one person can have toward another is that of conditional worth. Some examples are:

- I will love you *if* you get good grades.
- I will value you *if* you take care of my needs.
- You can have scholastic freedom *if* you use our interpretative framework.
- You can pastor our church *if* you are not a woman.

A climate of conditional love can inhibit personal growth, stifle creativity, and cause fear. I am not giving sanction to a permissiveness that does not have biblical boundaries for acceptable and unacceptable beliefs. The Scriptures are clear in matters of faith and practice. It is the peripheral issues, the formulation of theologies (synthesis), the application of Scripture, and matters where there is no certain word (e.g., the form of church government) that we need to be open and accepting toward each other. It is only in an environment of acceptance that we can explore personal or group biases that inhibit the accurate and useful interpretation of the Bible. Both the church and psychotherapy provide a context for such acceptance.

Caring Enough to Confront

Most of us will agree that it is easier to be confronted by a person who accepts us. "Speaking the truth in love" is therefore central to the revelation of our biases. We need prophets who speak the Word of God to us, but often hear only prophets who accept us in love. Hosea and Amos declared the Word of God to a nation loved by God. It took courage to declare an unpopular message. Prophets need to be people of courage, and at times they will be unpopular. By all means we must hear their message. A theological movement, church body, and even a nation that silences or ignores its prophets stands in great peril. Prophets are threatening to the status quo, but they cannot be a law unto themselves. They stand alone, but not unaccountable. The meaning of Scripture is their point of reference and accountability. They are prophets of the Word of God and should speak from a multicultural perspective.

Another area where there needs to be both cooperation and confrontation reflects multicultural concerns. Charles Taber reflecting on the necessity of such a church venture writes:

> There is need for continual cross-fertilization and mutual correction and I expect that a genuinely Asian or African theology will develop insights unavailable to unaided Western

theology, but which can in varying degrees be communicated to Westerners to their spiritual enrichment. [13]

The effective prophet is therefore a Christian with a world-wide perspective. The Bible informs this perspective, and the prophet must maintain the delicate balance between freedom and responsibility.

Someone once said of the moral environment in the United States that the Statue of Liberty in the East should have a counterpart in the West, the Statue of Responsibility. The one essential factor in the realization of the creative artist or prophet is freedom. Paul affirms freedom in Christ as a norm for Christian living: "It is for freedom that Christ has set us free. Stand firm, then, and do not let yourselves be burdened again by a yoke of slavery" (Gal. 5:1). Does the church give biblical interpreters this freedom? The discussion above shows that the group does sometimes inhibit paradigmatic change. The truly creative artist/scientist is sometimes forced to look over his or her shoulder and ask, "What does the group think of my interpretation?" Must the interpreter remain a victim of this group-imposed bondage? No; each one of us may take the responsibility to declare our own carefully considered, although sometimes myopic, interpretative perspectives. Freedom is something we take for ourselves. The affirmation of such freedom, however, does not absolve the interpreter of responsibility to the group. There is a delicate balance between freedom and responsibility within the body of Christ.

The relationship between the church as a group and its individual interpreters can be compared to the relationship between God and His people in the Bible. It is a covenantal rather than a contractual relationship. God takes the initiative; He chooses us as His people. "I will be their God, and they will be my people" (2 Cor. 6:16).

109

Most relationships today are contractual rather than covenantal. Even modern marriage relationships tend to be contractually based, so that "quid pro quo" ("something for something") is understood in the vows, even when, "For better, for worse, for richer, for poorer . . ." is spoken. Thus also, the church tends to say to its interpreters, "Do things our way; interpret from our perspective, and in our tradition if you want our sanction." More freedom, creativity, and responsibility would result if the church would say, "We are committed to freedom, but we must also call each other to responsibility."

Contracts are made in the quest of security. Many have the notion that we need to nail each other down because human nature is basically untrustworthy. Having a contract is safer. The interpersonal stance in a covenantal relationship is more humble; each considers himself a servant to the other. Each is committed to the other even if it means disagreements over biblical interpretation that could threaten our security. We stand together as believers—for better, for worse. We are in a covenant relationship with God and with each other. The Bible is our ultimate standard of faith and practice.

Ultimately, however, there is no unbridled freedom of interpretation. The individual artist/scientist is responsible to God and His Word. Individuals are to submit to their leaders (Heb. 13:17) in the church, but there is a delicate balance between freedom and responsibility. The group pressure or desire regarding an interpretation is not the last word, and the surrender of personal interpretative freedom could be wrong for an individual.

And so the person seeks to responsibly interpret the Word with a personal sense of freedom. An accepting church is the ideal context. However, there is another powerful factor involved—the Spirit of God.

The Spirit and the Word

There are times when we may ask, What is truth? How can we know the meaning and application of this portion of Scripture? Such questions may arise in response to discussions of personal bias in interpretation. The statement of the perspicuity of Scripture may not assist the person who wrestles with such questions. What then?

The Bible itself speaks about the operation of the Spirit of God. He is the one who comes alongside the interpreter and helps him or her grasp the meaning and application of the Bible. Jesus speaks of the Holy Spirit as the one who "will guide you into all truth" (John 16:13). He says also that "the Spirit will take from what is mine and make it known to you" (John 16:15).

We can take great courage from reflection on such truths. The believer is indwelt by the Spirit of God who is active in revealing His word. The implications of the inner operations of the Holy Spirit for biblical interpretation are twofold:

1. As the Spirit of truth, He can assist us in the understanding and monitoring of our biases.
2. We can launch out in the creative interpretation of the Bible by allowing the Holy Spirit to work in our minds.

At all times the Spirit of God draws us back to the written Word of God and attests to its truthfulness. It is He who is active in revealing the Word to us and helping us extricate ourselves from personal and cultural biases. He also uses means other than the Bible. He may work through therapeutic relationships within the church— both informal and professional. At all times we can work on the assumption that He is active in revealing truth. He brings the Word alive to our darkened minds.

We invoke His assistance and allow Him to lead us into all truth.

CONCLUSION

The process of gaining insight to our fear is necessary for accurate biblical interpretation. We need to free ourselves of the bondage of wanting to please ourselves and others at the expense of truth. Unless we break the shackles of fear we will continue to be biased in our interpretation of Scripture. We need the courage of the prophets, the acceptance of the church, the assistance of the Holy Spirit, and the gentle confrontations manifested in a variety of therapeutic relationships. We may never have a full and complete knowledge of the meaning and application of the Bible, but recognizing and dealing with our innate biases and fears while calling upon the supportive community of the church and the guidance of the Spirit will make us better able to interpret God's Word.

NOTES

[1]Kahil Gibran, *Thoughts and Meditations* (Secaucus, N.J.: Citadel, 1973), p. 31.

[2]Ernest Becker, *The Denial of Death* (New York: The Free Press, 1973), p. 76.

[3]Ibid., p. 78.

[4]J. Gillies, *My Needs, Your Needs, Our Needs* (Bergenfield, N.J.: New American Library, 1974), p. 6.

[5]F. Perls, *Gestalt Therapy Verbatim* (Moab, Utah: Real People Press, 1969), p. 4.

[6]K. Barth, *Dogmatics in Outline* (London: Camelot, 1960), p. 10.

[7]K. Gibran, *The Prophet* (New York: Knopf, 1968), p. 7.

[8]R. K. Johnston, *Evangelicals at an Impasse* (Atlanta: John Knox, 1979), p. 152.

[9]C. Taber, "Is There More Than One Way to do Theology?" *Gospel in Context,* January 1978, p. 10.

[10]M. Noll "Who Sets the Stage for Understanding Scripture?" *Christianity Today,* May 1980, pp. 14–18.

[11]James Woelfel, "The Personal Dimension in Theological Enquiry, En-

counter," *Creative Theological Scholarship,* Summer 1981, p. 232.

[12]Clinton McLemore, *The Scandal of Psychotherapy* (Wheaton: Tyndale, 1982).

[13]Taber, "Is There More than One Way to do Psychotherapy?", p. 10.

CONCLUSION

The journey into the psychology of biblical interpretation has taken us to the polar extremes of human bias that obscures the message and the resourcefulness of the mind in discerning truth. There are differences in interpretation within evangelical Christianity and between major sections of the historical church. No one has the corner on the truth. There will always be differences in interpretation. Human bias, conditioned by personal and social environments, will always be evident. Our task is to monitor and compensate for such bias.

Biblical scholars and lay interpreters alike have suspected that there was more to interpretation than grammatical-historical research. In the basic research of exegesis, as long as the rules of hermeneutics are followed, there is little ambiguity of meaning. It is when we get beyond exegesis to synthesis and application that we begin to theologize. Theology is an interpretative discipline that systematizes the data. There are "clear" truths in Scripture discoverable by all who would, in the strength of the Spirit, search diligently. The Bible is sufficiently clear for faith and salvation. We must, however, make a distinction between peripheral and central issues. There are large areas of agreement among Evangelicals; these include: the Virgin Birth of Christ, the need for personal faith in Christ, and the death and Resurrection of the Lord. Within certain doctrines there are both differences and agreements on major issues. For instance, there is agreement on aspects of the personal return of Christ but a variety of opinions on the timing of the Rapture.

No matter what truth we seek to discern in Scripture our minds are involved in the formulation of theories. We don't just stumble on truth that awaits our explorations. Our mental theorizing involves the classification of things in the light of antecedent preconceptions and expectations. "Pure" observation does not exist. Our minds are always guided by anticipatory theories; hypotheses are formed as a result of the creative exercise of our imagination. Sometimes this creative process contaminates or distorts, sometimes it clarifies the truth of the Bible. Sometimes our theological models are accurate and sometimes they are not. They are never complete. Some models undergo revision but retain their essential form. The church councils of Nicea and Calcedon are still speaking to the modern church on the nature and work of Christ. The reason such models have abiding value is that they are true to the meaning of Scripture. Other theological models based on philosophical trends lose their significance after a relatively short period. Examples of the latter include the death-of-God theology, process theology, and existentialism.

Some models of hermeneutics and theology undergo change through the process of accommodation and paradigm shift. Covenant and dispensational theologies are examples of such changes. In all cases of change of theological models the human mind creatively involves itself with the divinely given meaning. Creativity can be the crown we wear as well as the cross we bear, especially when it comes to the synthesis and application of meaning.

Too often with Evangelicalism there is an emotional and political commitment to incomplete theological and hermeneutical models. Creative prophets are silenced, ostracized, or paternalistically tolerated. Fear of such responses cause many a prophet to surrender critical judgment for the sake of acceptance in the group. This book hopes to call such prophets to courage, creative interpretation, and assertiveness. Women called to the ministry and gifted accordingly should not despair. What does a present-day prophet do when an ecclesiastical constituency will not tolerate a new position? There are no easy solutions. Each must travel a lonely road, but we cannot ultimately allow what others think and feel cause us to deny what we really believe for ourselves.

It is painful to stand alone in a constituency that is sold on an incomplete model of interpretation. H. G. Wells poignantly wrote of the dangers and pain associated with social conformity in *Country of the Blind,* where he tells of a group of people in South America cut off from civilization by a natural disaster. For many generations they lived in isolation. With each successive generation the children born into this group became less sighted. After a period, the whole group was blind. They adapted so well to the blindness that eventually nobody noticed the loss. One day a stranger, Nunez, on a mountaineering expedition from Bogota, was caught in a landslide and fell into the valley and was discovered by the blind settlers. Nunez thought that he was at an advantage with the blind people and attempted to get them to acknowledge his superiority. He comments to the leader, "Has no one told you 'In the country of the blind the one-eyed man is king?'" "What is blind?" asked the blind man casually.[1]

When Nunez fell in love with one of the young women in the valley and wished to marry her, he was faced with the terrible choice—have himself blinded or relinquish his love. The group did not want him to be a misfit. He wanted to marry his love but also be accepted as he was by the community. Their value system dictated that sightedness was to be equated with sickness. It took all his strength to leave the happy valley and his love in order to retain his sight. This symbolic story has been repeated hundreds of times in the field of interpretation and theology. Some interpreters choose to retain their sight. Others, however, allow their eyes to be put out for the sake of the acceptance of their beloved people.

It is not just the group that silences creativity but the inner fear of the prophet. No one can say, "The group made me silent," just as we cannot blame the devil for causing us to sin. We are all personally responsible for what we do with the light we receive. We are also responsible for discovering how our personal biases distort our understanding of the meaning and significance of the Scriptures. Sheldon Kopp writes: "Being on our own, each of us must take personal responsibility of coming to know the wolf within or we risk becoming the lamb that slaughters the rest of the flock."[2]

We dare not view our inner psyches and biases like the parent who says of the child in the band, "Look, my son is the only one in step. All the others led off with the wrong foot!" Our unconscious mental sets and responses can interfere with the quest for the meaning of the Scripture. A psychotherapeutic relationship, the prayer closet, the community of believers, the inner activity of the Holy Spirit, and the Bible itself provide the necessary correctives for personal bias. The journey toward insight into our biases must be followed by the exercise of personal responsibility in response to the discovered meaning. It is an important journey since it is foundational to our lives. We must know the meaning of the Word before it can be profitable for all aspects of life. We must not choose to give our lives for vaporous models of meaning. The Lord intends that we know the truth that sets us free. Such knowing is a process to which all pilgrims are called. The journey traveled by theologian and behavioral scientists, hopefully together, is always under the authority of the Scriptures and the guidance of the Spirit of God.

NOTES

[1]H. G. Wells, "The Country of the Blind," in *The Complete Short Stories of H. G. Wells* (London: Ernest Benn, 1927), p. 179.

[2]Sheldon Kopp, *An End to Innocence* (New York: Bantam, 1978), p. 2.